Praise for *Reclaim Regret*

"If you are burdened with regret and feel that you must live with the pain, this is the book for you. Sr. Kathryn will show you a path toward healing."

—Timothy M. Gallagher, OMV, author of *The Discernment of Spirits: An Ignatian Guide to Everyday Living*

"Some books are to be read, others savored. This book offers us a banquet of scriptural truths and transformative experiences leading readers to taste and see the goodness of the Lord. It illuminates in personal and practical ways the paradoxical reality that in every limit there is a blessing in disguise, that in every regret there is a reason for hope."

—Susan Muto, PhD, Dean of Epiphany Academy of Formative Spirituality

"This practical, hope-filled book is beautifully written and full of wisdom gleaned from ~~~~~ nal experience and minis~~~~~ n serves as a trustworth~~~~~ heart of God and then i~~~~~ to read this book with~~~~~ the healing meditations that make up the second part of the book. As you do, you will engage in a process of deep soul healing, releasing the regrets and disappointments that have prevented you from living the fullness of joy that Jesus promises."

—Bob Schuchts, founder of John Paul II Healing Center, Tallahassee, Florida, and author of *Be Healed: A Guide to Encountering the Powerful Love of Jesus in Your Life*

"With utter confidence in God's abiding love, Sr. Kathryn deftly guides her readers on a healing journey, transforming regrets into life-giving possibilities."

—Mark Neilsen, writer and former editor of *Living Faith: Daily Catholic Devotions*

"Words don't change hearts; grace does. But these words of Sr. Hermes facilitate grace in a powerful way. With great insight, she has tapped into what wounds the human heart, and she shows, as if by intimate knowledge, the ways of a Loving Father who desires to heal. Read these words, practice the exercises, and let your heart be healed."

—Dr. Gregory Bottaro, director of the CatholicPsych Institute, and author of *The Mindful Catholic: Finding God One Moment at a Time*

"The best of contemporary spiritual and psychological wisdom, this accessible and powerfully experiential book will heal not only you, but your relationships as well. If I had one gift to bequeath my children, it would be to reclaim regret."

—Denise DeSesa-Smith, PhD, Licensed Psychologist

"A beautiful, inspirational guide with universal appeal, teaching us how to live with and accept our regrets, and then move on, feeling our burdens have been lifted . . ."

—Fred Silverstone, Psychotherapist and
Licensed Mental Health Counselor

"In *Reclaim Regret*, Sr. Kathryn weaves Scripture, regrets, and prayer into heart-transforming experiences, using an authentic, clear, and compassionate style of writing. My journey of repentance, transformation, and living a new life in Christ has been supported and enhanced one hundredfold."

—Mary Celine Weidenbenner, OSU, teacher at
Mary Carrico Catholic School in Knottsville, Kentucky

RECLAIM REGRET

RECLAIM REGRET

HOW GOD HEALS LIFE'S DISAPPOINTMENTS

By Kathryn J. Hermes, FSP

BOOKS & MEDIA
Boston

Library of Congress Cataloging-in-Publication Data

Names: Hermes, Kathryn, author.

Title: Reclaim regret : how God heals life's disappointments / written by Kathryn J. Hermes, FSP.

Description: Boston : Pauline Books & Media, 2018. | Includes bibliographical references.

Identifiers: LCCN 2018002134| ISBN 9780819865137 (pbk.) | ISBN 0819865133 (pbk.)

Subjects: LCSH: Consolation. | Disappointment--Religious aspects--Christianity. | Regret--Religious aspects--Christianity. | Healing--Religious aspects--Christianity.

Classification: LCC BV4905.3 .H4725 2018 | DDC 248.8/6--dc23

LC record available at https://lccn.loc.gov/2018002134

Many manufacturers and sellers distinguish their products through the use of trademarks. Any trademarked designations that appear in this book are used in good faith but are not authorized by, associated with, or sponsored by the trademark owners.

Unless otherwise noted, the Scripture quotations contained herein are from the *New Revised Standard Version Bible: Catholic Edition,* copyright © 1989, 1993, Division of Christian Education of the National Council of the Churches of Christ in the United States of America. Used by permission. All rights reserved.

Other Scripture texts in this work are taken from the *New American Bible, Revised Edition* © 2010, 1991, 1986, 1970 Confraternity of Christian Doctrine, Washington, D.C. and are used by permission of the copyright owner. All Rights Reserved. No part of the *New American Bible* may be reproduced in any form without permission in writing from the copyright owner.

Cover design by Rosana Usselmann

Cover photo: Kintsugi art on cover is made by Morty Bachar, Lakeside Pottery Studio.

Published by Pauline Books & Media, 50 Saint Pauls Avenue, Boston, MA 02130-3491

Printed in the U.S.A.

www.pauline.org

Pauline Books & Media is the publishing house of the Daughters of St. Paul, an international congregation of women religious serving the Church with the communications media.

1 2 3 4 5 6 7 8 9   22 21 20 19 18

Contents

BOOK ONE

BOOK TWO

Foreword

You might be wondering about the meaning of this book's stunning cover and the beautifully repaired piece of pottery on it that has no doubt caught your eye. *Kintsugi* is the Japanese art of repairing ceramic with lacquer mixed with powdered gold, silver, or platinum. The bright golden lines visibly incorporate the repair into the piece emphasizing newness. Rather than disguising the brokenness, the radiant repairs help us to see the breakage as part of the history and beauty of the pottery that has been made whole again.

Reclaim Regret speaks to the brokenness that all of us experience at one time or another because of unresolved regrets. But, it's much more than that. This book provides a way to reflect on our hurts and to heal from them. Most of us, at some point, feel stuck in our lives due to past experiences. We might fear moving forward or we might believe that moving past something is impossible. Yet, we often can't *quite* figure out what is wrong, why we feel this way, and why our attempts to feel happy and to move forward have continued to fail.

The process of healing from regret is even further complicated by the fact that most of us are very busy. We are unable to take the time to reflect on our past because we are up to our elbows in unending projects and mired in a constant effort to check off endless to-do lists. We feel the need to keep up, and we are just too busy to take the time to examine the problem. I would even venture to say that some of us operate in this kind of survival mode for many years, perhaps because we are purposefully trying to forget something painful, or more specifically, our haunting regrets.

We attempt to get by, to survive by maintaining the hectic, numbing pace of our lives. But while we are keeping so busy, suddenly something happens that makes us take stock of our lives. As the author, Sr. Kathryn Hermes, puts it in the introduction: "Something happens. You are stopped in your tracks." She lists a myriad of scenarios that can cause this to occur and explains, "As you absorb the pain of what is happening, the important things begin to surface." That's when the "could haves" and "should haves" begin to spin around in our brains. As we begin to grapple with the weight and reality of our regrets, we might be surprised by sudden agonizing pain. We might not know where to turn and feel so overwhelmed that we try to stuff the uncomfortable feelings back down inside to deal with at another time—or possibly never.

However, to find a healthy balance in our lives, we all must face our regrets with God's help at some point. Every single one of us experiences regret. As Sr. Kathryn points out, "Regret comes in all shapes and sizes." When we feel overcome by regret, we might ask ourselves some of the following questions: "What can I do with all of the new questions that have surfaced as a result of a traumatic event?" or "What can I do when I am jolted by an event that forces me to reflect upon the evocative past?" or "What can I do with the self doubt and the thoughts that haunt me?" And most importantly, "What role can my faith play in this process of healing from my regret?"

I know without a doubt that faith has played an indispensable role in my life. I wrote about my crooked path in my spiritual memoir *The Kiss of Jesus: How Mother Teresa and the Saints Helped Me to Discover the Beauty of the Cross* (Ignatius Press). When I encountered difficulties, abuse, and uncertainties in my life, the beautiful virtue of faith kept me moving forward—one step at a time. I have learned from personal experience that we are meant to turn to the virtues of faith, hope, and love when we experience pain and regret. The theological virtues are like muscles that need to be flexed and nourished. When we face regret, we need to pray for an increase in these virtues because we need God's help to heal.

Sr. Kathryn skillfully shows us how to enter into this healing process with courage. She also reminds us that healing from our regrets is the same as entering into "the amazing mystery of God's love." In *Reclaim Regret*, Sr. Kathryn takes us gently by the hand and helps us through the steps of healing so that we might experience God's beautiful promise of newness. Through modern-day stories, Scripture, Church teaching, and concrete exercises, this book leads readers through a process that will end in the discovery of great hope in the midst of sometimes agonizing regrets. With the help of Sr. Kathryn's astute insights and God's healing grace, all your painful mistakes, abuse, or hurts can be transformed. With God's help, *Reclaim Regret* can help us all to embrace our own unique lives and to be at peace.

DONNA-MARIE COOPER O'BOYLE

author and EWTN TV host

Acknowledgments

I want to express my gratitude to God, who has allowed me to walk with many different people along the path of finding hope in the midst of regrets. For those who have entrusted me with their hearts' work, I thank you. I also owe a debt of gratitude to Sr. Maria Grace Dateno, FSP, for believing in this project; and to Sr. Theresa Aletheia Noble, FSP, who had the vision and editorial skill to bring it to life.

The stories in this book have been inspired by the people who have entrusted some of their darkest memories and regrets to me over the years. Their stories have been blended together and names are changed for the sake of privacy.

Introduction

You are busy. Life happens. You can barely keep up. You know that you could be thinking about or doing more important things, but you don't have the time to stop and consider what they would be, much less do them.

And then something happens. You are stopped in your tracks. A spouse leaves. A friend dies. A job is lost. Opportunities pass you by. A child makes decisions that break your heart. As you absorb the pain of what is happening, the important things begin to surface. What was hidden suddenly seems so obvious. The knowledge of what you could have done, should have done, for years perhaps, or years ago, leaves you feeling profoundly empty, or guilty, or depressed.

If only you could do things over again . . .

Regrets come in all shapes and sizes. Navigating the questions, self-doubt, and haunting what-ifs of your life can be difficult. Facing how your regrets may have turned you into a person you never wanted to be is even more difficult. Yet no one escapes this part of life. It's the nightfall between yesterday and tomorrow, between the past and the future, between sunset and the coming dawn.

You may feel bad about something in your life that has happened to you or someone you love. You may be blaming yourself for a number of things. Perhaps you have given up hope that you will ever be able to retrieve what you have lost in life or fix what has been broken. A woman once shared with me that she still wonders what she did wrong after her marriage ended in divorce over twenty years ago. To this day, she wishes she could go to bed and never wake up. She is not alone in her suffering.

Through a program I designed called HeartWork, I have worked one-on-one with many people haunted by regrets. The people I have worked with often believe that if they had *just one more chance* things would be different, but they also feel that there are no more chances. But God always offers more chances. And this book provides you with the chance to return to explore what you regret in order to discover a new outcome.

This may seem impossible, but we have an amazing example of this right in the Scriptures. In the familiar story of Moses in the Book of Exodus, we read about an Israelite boy born in Egypt who was miraculously saved from slaughter by Pharaoh's daughter. Raised in Pharaoh's courts, Moses was expected to rise to power. But when he intervened on behalf of a kinsman and murdered an Egyptian, Moses became a fugitive. He fled Egypt to Midian where he met and married his wife, Zipporah. The man who once had been accustomed to the wealth of Pharaoh's household began tending his father-in-law flocks.

One day, as Moses was herding his sheep in the wilderness, he noticed a bush on fire but not burning up. As he moved closer to the curious sight, the Lord spoke to him, "Come no closer! Remove the sandals from your feet, for the place on which you are standing is holy ground" (Ex 3:4–5). The Lord then told Moses to return to Egypt to rescue the Israelites from oppression. Moses, however, was in no hurry to go back to Egypt. Most likely, he had already spent many long years reflecting on what had gone wrong. Perhaps he asked himself if he had already thwarted God's plan. He must have struggled with many regrets, what-ifs, and self-doubts.

But while Moses' face looked to the past, God's face looked to the future. When the Lord spoke to Moses from the burning bush, he could have pointed out Moses' mistakes in Egypt. Instead, God did not talk about the past. He already knew that Moses was well aware of his mistakes. So he told Moses he was sending him back to Egypt with a message for Pharaoh. The Lord was revealing a future to Moses that would pass right through the center of what he most feared. In some mysterious way, on that day before the burning bush, Moses received back all he thought he had lost.

You too are standing on holy ground. This book invites you to take off your sandals for a while and experience holy ground—*your* holy ground!

I have had the privilege of working extensively with people struggling with broken hearts and guilt over the things that have happened in their lives—things done *to* them and things done *by* them. I often share with them what I have learned in my own struggle with regrets, and my experience walking through my regrets often helps them to find hope.

You have not made this journey yet, so you may have trouble believing that a light shines on the other side of the darkness of regret. But I can tell you from experience that it does. God wants to heal your heart and bring you into the light of his love.

God makes four promises to the person haunted with regrets:

○ *First Promise:* I want to throw you a party.

○ *Second Promise:* Look at me, and you will know who you are.

○ *Third Promise:* You see your failure, I see your future.

○ *Fourth Promise:* My light will radiate from you for all the world to see.

These promises that begin each part in Book One are deeply rooted in Scripture and offer a concrete framework for healing. Book One will provide you with different tools to help you face your regrets, bring them to God, and find healing. The promises are not based on my human abilities as an author and spiritual counselor, but on God's divine abilities, on God, who heals life's disappointments.

Presented along with God's promises are skills that you can learn to attain personal development and spiritual growth. Each of these skills will help you to reclaim your regret in the light of God's love so that new life can blossom.

Some of the skills you will learn are to:

○ uncover destructive patterns in your life;

○ free yourself from the memories and fears that plague you;

○ get in touch with your pain and embrace your life as it really is;

○ stop building your life around your regrets;

○ hold the memories of all you regret with reverence;

○ learn how to entrust the *mystery* of your future to the Lord.

After gaining the tools and skills in Book One, and meditating on God's never-ending love for you, Book Two invites you to continue to bring to prayer all of your regrets and struggles through meditations. The meditations are general enough to help anyone struggling with regrets but specific enough that you will find help for all that haunts you.

Rest assured that following the course of action in this book will help you to discover that your regrets are holy ground—*your* holy ground!

So, come with me on a journey *into* yourself. Movement, change, shadows, discoveries—you will find all of these things as you go. This book will take you through forgotten memories and into unfamiliar emotional territory. Welcome and attend to everything that comes up along the way. There is no "wrong" emotion to feel in this process. Embrace whatever comes up and surrender it to Jesus. At some points you may feel more burdened than you did before, but trust that this journey will ultimately lead to more clarity, lighten your load, and bless you.

Your regrets are holy ground— *your* holy ground!

A piece of advice. Simply reading this book will not lead you to healing. You can't make a trip somewhere by just reading about it. Spiritual journeys are not logical expositions. They are messy things of the heart. This journey through your regrets to peace will be like going up a mountain. Just as mountain roads don't lead straight to the top but circle around to the summit gradually, in the same way, the material in this book will lead you on a gentle, gradual, cyclical journey. This book presents the same kind of material in each section, but each time with a new twist and with deeper spiritual lessons. Also, when you get to Book Two, you may feel tempted to skip over it or read quickly through it. Resist the temptation! The most important parts of this book are the prayers and exercises in Books One and Two that will help you to encounter God. I urge you to give them the time they—and you—deserve. Bringing this process to prayer will absolutely be key to your healing process.

Finally, dear reader, have courage! Journeys often involve detours, surprises, new information, rest stops, traffic jams, and unexpected experiences. In fact, so you can't take logical control of the journey, surprises and unexpected experiences are built into this book. But I promise, if you put yourself into the meditations and stories and take time with each exercise, you *will* discover the incredible beauty of God's promises to all of us human beings. We are flawed, yes, but oh so incredibly loved!

BOOK ONE

PART ONE

God's First Promise to You

I want to throw you a party.

"Let us eat and celebrate; for this son of mine was
dead and is alive again; he was lost and is found!"

— Luke 15:23–24

Regrets can haunt your memories and make you feel bad about yourself—somehow less worthy. You may blame yourself for many things: roads not taken, opportunities missed, and dreams that have slipped away. Perhaps an inability to overcome your problems or fix your mistakes is discouraging you. This part of the book will show you how to uncover destructive patterns in your life so that God can intervene to establish something new.

CHAPTER ONE

"My son . . . everything I have is yours."

"You know my Dad," said the roughly dressed young man to a field hand as they walked together to the edge of the vast property to fix fences. The young man began to open a gate, but then he suddenly spun around and slammed it shut. The fence shuddered under the impact of his anger. "He takes me for granted and spoils my younger brother," he yelled. "Always his 'younger son.' Never the rest of his family. Never *me*."

The field hand was used to this daily tirade and had learned to tune it out. After all, this son, the only son their employer had left, worked hard and was fair to all the workers. They had it good, and for that they were grateful. He could put up with the complaining.

The young man turned around one last time before they walked around the road's bend that would hide the house from their view. He saw his broken-hearted father standing in the road, grieving for his runaway son—watching, hoping, waiting—somehow staunchly refusing to give up hope. "Who knows where my brother is," the elder son muttered under his breath. "I wish he knew how much he's devastated this family. He took a third of our assets, liquidated in a matter of days so he could take off with the money and waste it all. I hope he's happy, wherever he is."

The father turned and watched his eldest son disappear down the road. He thanked God for this son who was so consistent and dependable. The father wished his eldest son realized how much he loved him. He didn't know what he could do to help him see that he loved *both* his sons. Turning back, he gazed off into the distance, hoping to see his runaway son. "If only you'd come home, my son. . . . How my heart longs to see your face here again. If only the family could be whole once more." Shaking his head, he returned to the shade of the house.

The aging father eventually started to doze off in the heat of the day. Suddenly, he jerked awake and settled his eyes on the ever-empty road. *Wait—what was that moving in the distance?* He squinted in the sunlight and shielded his eyes. No one ever walked the road at this time of the day. Ever. What was that . . . or . . . *who* was that? It almost looked like someone walking. His heart began to quicken as he stood up. Walking slowly down the road, he strained his eyes to see. *Don't get excited,* he told himself, trying to keep himself steady. *Be sure.* But his heart more certain than his sight, he began to hurry toward the moving figure walking along the side of the road. He felt his heart almost reaching out to the heart of the person walking his way with head down. But, the clothes, the height, the gait . . . yes, this was *his* son.

How the father's heart pitied him. He was not returning in triumph. Something had gone wrong. The father began to run toward him, calling his boy's name, laughing to himself with delight, relieved. As he came closer, his son saw him and stopped. The older man quickly closed the distance between them, calling out his son's name again and again. "My son, I knew one day I would see you again. My son, come here."

They stood before each other, the father ecstatic, the son ashamed, his eyes downcast. "My son! Look at me! I knew I'd live to see this day! I knew you'd come back to me!"

"Father, no, I need to apologize," the son protested.

"My son!"

"No. I have sinned against heaven and against you." The son had prepared a speech. He was ready to work as a farmhand, to pay back his debt, the inheritance he had lost. *What I did was wrong. If you only knew where I've been and what I've done since I left. I'm so ashamed. If you'd just let me live with the hired hands. . . .* But he choked on the words. As the Father embraced him again and again, the son finally understood just how much he had broken his father's heart. *My father still loves me, has always loved me. How can this be?* He realized at last that while he had lost his inheritance, he still had a relationship with his father who loved him. He had not understood.

The father looked at his disheveled, dirty, and ashamed son. He could only imagine where he had been. He saw that at last the boy didn't have his own plans anymore, that he had a sense of his father's love for him, and in that moment he chose to show his son the plans of his loving mercy. Softly he said to the boy, "You're my *son*. Always my son. . . ."

"But . . ."

"No." It was a firm but compassionate command. "I've waited for you every day. I've waited for my *son*. And now my son is here. I'll put a ring on your finger because you are a part of the family, not a hired hand. You have a permanent place in the family. You're always welcome here." Calling to a servant, the father asked that a feast be prepared so that he could celebrate that, at last, he had his son again.

Later in the day, the banquet had barely begun when a servant came running in with a message for the father: "Your oldest son is outside fuming with anger. He refuses to come in." The news, though whispered, rippled through the festive gathering. The youngest son stiffened. He was afraid of this. He looked at his father who had just been publicly insulted.

"I hope he punishes that boy!" one of the guests whispered.

"How sad. What a humiliation!" another person said quietly. As the father rose to go find his angry oldest boy outside, the guests murmured, shocked that the father would go out to his son after such a dishonor.

As soon as the father stepped out of the house, his elder son exclaimed, "What do you think you're doing reconciling with my no-good brother who's devoured a third of our property doing who-knows-what? What about me? What about throwing a party for me, since you're such a good father? I've slaved for you all these years!"

The father closed his eyes. *I've slaved for you. . . . So that's it,* he thought. *Slaving away, a servant, not a son, not love. My son acknowledges no relationship with his brother, with me.* Slowly he started to speak, eyes still closed, "Son." A pause. "Son, everything I have is yours. Your inheritance is still here, still yours. You know that. But my greatest desire, that I would one day see my youngest son again—your brother—has been fulfilled. He's home. How could I not rejoice after my prayers had been answered?"

— Meditation based on Luke 15:11–32

Prayer Moment

Praying with the stories of the Gospel heals hearts. Here is a simple guide to entering deeply into Scripture by using your imagination to place yourself in the events. If it is helpful, feel free to come back to this page whenever you meditate with the Scripture stories throughout the book.

1. Remember that you are a temple of the Holy Spirit, and take a moment to silently pray for light and guidance. If you have a specific regret, offer it to the Holy Spirit before reading Scripture.

2   Slowly read Luke 15:11–32.

3. Read the passage a second time and, as you do, try to picture what is happening and to imagine what each of the characters in the passage might be feeling. Enter into their experience as God leads you.

4. After spending a few moments in silence, notice a word, phrase, detail, or attitude of a character in the Scripture passage that speaks to you the most.

5. Then, read and pray with the guided meditation that follows and let yourself be led.

Both the elder and younger son had regrets. They were running away from something in themselves or from the way their lives had turned out. When have you felt this way?

At some point … we all find ourselves starving for God's *mercy*.

Each of *us* is a runaway in some part of our lives. Since Adam and Eve, it is part of the human condition to seek one's own way. To a greater or lesser degree, perhaps you have taken things into your own hands and have sought to build a life for yourself outside of God's will. Have you looked out for number one, not trusting God to take care of your best interests? At some point in our journey away from God, we all find ourselves starving for God's mercy.

Have you started the journey home?

STEP ONE

Imagine yourself as the runaway son, returning home at the lowest point in your life. Don't think about him, watch him, or pray about him. Instead, enter into his experience. *Feel* what he felt. He felt like a failure. What was he thinking? He had squandered all that his father had given him. What did he expect from his father? How did he feel about himself?

Step Two

Then imagine yourself as the older son—put out, angry with the way life has unfolded, jealous of what others have. He was tired from all the work, others' expectations, and other people's failure to step up to the plate.

Step Three

Merge with the younger son being received by the father. Play his role in the parable story. Imagine yourself approaching your father. When you look at him you can see that he knows your pain, all your inner suffering. He reaches out to you, holding his arms open. He looks into your eyes. What do you see? What does the father say to you? Put yourself in the scene as the father puts a ring on your finger and restores you, his lost child, to the status of an honored and respected son or daughter.

Step Four

Imagine a party being thrown for you in heaven. Jesus approaches you with his arms wide open. What is that like for you? What does he say to you? Allow yourself to feel the full texture of the experience.

———◇—◇———

When we use our imagination to pray with Scripture, we can be profoundly moved by grace. We might notice new insights, new desires, or a shift that we can't quite explain or deny. What new insights do you notice? How is God moving your heart? What new perspective do you have on a situation in your life? How do you feel God calling you to respond differently to him or to others? How have you experienced God's love in a new way?

CHAPTER TWO

Discover the Patterns
of Regret in Your Life

Jake looked out the window of his house. The beauty of the spring day sharply contrasted with the silent, drab, and almost empty rooms around him. Jake was waiting for his daughter Suzanne to arrive. He could hardly believe she would graduate from high school in another year. He was so proud of her. She was at the top of her class, interesting, beautiful, curious, and compassionate. Suzanne was the only one of Jake's children who still showed any interest in seeing him.

Three years had passed since Jake's wife, Sarah, had told him to leave. He wondered how he could have missed the signals that they were growing apart. Now Jake lived alone near his family in case anyone ever wanted to visit him. But, unless his other two sons and daughter needed money, Jake only regularly saw Suzanne.

I met Jake in California and we met over the course of a year for HeartWork sessions. A broken man in his mid-forties, Jake cried with agonizing sobs for the first two months we met. The loss of his family and the remorse he felt for how he had raised his children greatly burdened him. "I've failed as a father." This phrase wove its way through every conversation and ground down his self-respect each time he repeated it.

Jake's father, a successful yet cold and distant man, had left the family when Jake was twelve. His alcoholic mother had suffered from depression for as long as he could remember. Jake had wanted to be there for his children because his parents had not been there for him. So Jake had focused all his energy on his four children, encouraging, monitoring, correcting, and doing everything he could to help them succeed.

Jake never attended college and, without any specialized skills, his job opportunities had been limited. When Jake and Sarah had married, his lack of education had not been an issue. Sarah was happy with her career and was in love with him. But with the birth of each child, their differences became more accentuated. Jake couldn't understand Sarah's more relaxed approach to parenting. To Jake, Sarah seemed unconcerned about the children's future. Sarah tried to explain that she just trusted the kids would make their own way in life, but Jake was unconvinced. Their arguments grew more frequent, especially after the children began school.

As Jake became more and more aware of his own responsibility in the break-up of his family, his heart ached with regret. Suffering with an undiagnosed mental illness, he had been a well-intentioned but somewhat volatile parent. Looking back, Jake could see how he had smothered his kids, not with affection but with demands. He wished he had focused more on developing relationships with his children than on their success, but he had wanted so much for them. And now he had lost them all. His family had left him behind, except for Suzanne.

"Why do you want to see me?" Jake would ask Suzanne, astounded that someone in his family wanted to spend time with him.

"Because you are my dad," Suzanne would respond simply.

The reestablished connection with his daughter began to heal Jake's soul.

One day, Jake arrived a few moments early to the parish where he attended Mass as often as he could. As he knelt before the Blessed Sacrament, a message unexpectedly reverberated in his heart: "Take off your shoes, this is holy ground." The words seemed commanding, almost audible. Jake didn't move; he knelt frozen in time. He held onto the moment as the meaning of the message washed over him. When Mass began, Jake rose with the assembly, and the mystery of the moment seemed to pass.

Later that week, near the end of our time together, Jake casually brought up to me what he had experienced before Mass. "It isn't that just the church is holy ground," Jake explained. "Every place is holy ground. God is everywhere. I felt all my problems slip away, as if they were dropping off my shoulders."

The Father had come down the road to meet him!

"Jake," I responded softly, "God just showed you his face. How did you feel when God spoke to you, when you heard those words?"

Jake sat in silence, reviving the embers of this fire so that its warmth might fill him once more. "I felt light, free, happy," he finally said quietly.

Through experiences like this, God imprints his seal on us, dynamically refashioning the deepest levels of our being. Over several months Jake and I returned to this memory again and again—a sacred moment of God's revelation of his personal love for Jake. We explored what Jake described as a spiritual experience of freedom, a feeling of boundlessness, which seemed to approach the Infinite. Such memories—sacred memories—are foundational to the process of healing and need to be relished in prayer and gratitude. When we work to unravel the multiple layers of meaning in these experiences, it helps us to believe in the eyes that have seen us and the words that have saved us.

Facing Our Regrets in Life

At some point in life, in our younger or later years, we all do something or experience a situation that we truly regret. In our younger years, it is usually an individual situation, something we did, a decision we made, an experience we had, or an incident that has re-written the script of our life without our permission, such as an illness or accident. In our older years, we may feel uneasy as we recognize that a pattern of regret has stamped itself on our entire lifetime, creating an ocean of sorrow within and around us.

Each of us has arrived at the age we are now bearing many scars. Some of us have scars from an imperfect or even abusive family life, unkind teachers, envious siblings, or teenage romances that broke our hearts. Others have been wounded by employers who fired us, spouses who betrayed us, colleagues who took advantage of us, or children who were ungrateful. Our regrets are built on years of memories of hurts and disappointments, both intentional and accidental.

Some people may feel like victims of random situations or hurtful relationships. We don't know why things happen to us the way they do. Our lives don't match up with the seemingly magical lives of those around us, and we don't understand why. But the "random" situations in our life that we regret are anything but random. It is possible, and even liberating, to identify the recurring patterns that lay beneath our regrets.

The patterns beneath our regrets can be difficult to discover because, on the surface, every situation is unique. For example, consider Stacy, a woman with a successful career as a lawyer. She is a no-nonsense person who gets what she wants, regardless of how it may affect others. As a parent she challenges any negative feedback regarding her children. She pushed her oldest child to attend a top-rated college and to follow in her footsteps in the field of law. While Stacy acts differently in her career than in her parenting, we can see a similar pattern in both spheres. As a lawyer and a parent, Stacy tries to dominate and force others to do what she wants. In one sphere it might work, but in the other it causes Stacy serious problems and leads to broken relationships.

Scott is someone who finds his life frustrated by a series of failures that he always thinks another person caused. For every failure, Scott faults anyone but himself. When something goes wrong, Scott has fallen into the habit of shifting the blame and not taking responsibility. People who are close to Scott try to help him see the part he plays in his difficulties, but he is not open to feedback. But if Scott looked closely, he would realize that his own thoughts, beliefs, and responses play a part in this pattern of blame in his life.

Each of these unfortunate situations is unique because every one of us is unique and we experience the world differently. Yet our experiences often form a more general underlying pattern. Unless we make a concerted effort, we rarely discover these patterns, and when we can't see them, we are doomed to repeat them again and again in our lives.

Uncovering Patterns Will Help You Unravel Your Problems

As children we learned what we needed to do to get attention and love: be good, be an exceptional student, be the family clown, be the one who cares for the rest of the family, be just like mom or dad, or be there to listen to a parent's opinions, problems, or tears. And what we learned served us well at the time. However, as adults we often repeat that behavior in order to secure the love and attention we crave. So if we want to break free from these patterns, we have to uncover them in our lives.

In the earlier story, after meeting with Jake for many months, we gradually uncovered a lifelong pattern that had imposed itself on his attitudes, desires, and communication style. This pattern had propelled him to make decisions that on the surface seemed heroic—"I wanted to give my kids everything I didn't have." But lurking beneath Jake's decisions were unconscious needs that drove him to focus all of his energies on his children's success and to neglect the emotional needs of both his wife and his children.

Jake's earliest memories were of sitting at the dinner table and his parents shaming him for not being as smart as his brothers. When he described those memories, he said it felt like looking out a window and not being able to see anything. As we pieced his story together, Jake told me that when he was young he would always play with younger children rather than those of his own age. He would teach them how to play baseball and ride with them on the bike trail. His younger brother had once said that Jake was the only one in the family who cared about him. Jake's low sense of self-worth led him to replay this original pattern, established in his childhood. He continued to avoid relating to peers. He didn't cultivate friendships with anyone his age, but instead spent most of his time with his children.

Jake thought he was acting like a good father. "I loved my kids," Jake said. "I wanted to have a good relationship with them, like the one I always wished for with my own father but never had. And I didn't want them to get stuck in a dead-end job." He attended every baseball game his children played. He made sure they did their homework. Jake pushed them to excel and succeed, warning them that their life would turn out badly if they didn't prepare for their own future. But his children complained that they felt suffocated, and Sarah longed for the adult friendship and support that Jake didn't know how to give her. This dynamic, established in his childhood, replayed throughout his life. But it ultimately collapsed when Jake's wife told him to leave.

Little by little, Jake began to see the deeper pattern: *he* was the one who had desperately needed his *children's* love. He began to realize he had been using his children to satisfy unmet emotional needs from his childhood. But as a father, Jake's role was to give his children unconditional love. Now he regretted the years lost, the demands, arguments, and all the angry tirades. Now it seemed too late to restore what had been lost.

Although Jake's story led to extreme consequences, it is similar to the story we each have. Each one of us has patterns of behavior that lead us to behave in ways we often regret. If we do not become aware of these patterns, we often continually replay them in our lives. When regrets build upon one another, we can get to the point where we feel we will never get out from beneath them. But the first step, with God's grace, is to identify the patterns in our lives that lead us to make unhealthy decisions in the first place.

Exercise
Identify the Patterns in Your Life

When I was told that identifying patterns behind the things I regret in my life was a powerful way to make new choices for my future, I was skeptical. "Prove it," I said. But when I tried this little exercise, I began to clearly see some of the patterns that were influencing the circumstances in my life.

This is a foundational yet powerful exercise that you can do often. Each time you do it, powerful feelings from long ago can be processed and released. It won't happen all at once; it takes time. You may feel overwhelmed at first when you identify unhealthy patterns in your life, but this is only the first step. God will use the patterns of regrets that fill your heart as your teachers.

God will use the patterns of regrets that fill *your heart* as your teachers.

STEP ONE

Find a quiet place where you can think. Bring some writing paper or a favorite journal.

Step Two

After you settle down, think about your present life. Identify something in it that does not satisfy you. Look for a disappointment or a situation that makes you feel anger, envy, or fear.

Step Three

Once you identify that area, think about what your life was like ten years ago. What were you doing? What was happening? It helps to write down what you remember. It is likely you will discover that although you were living in a different situation, you had similar feelings about yourself or others. You might have responded in the same way, in the same tone of voice, with the same beliefs.

Step Four

Go back ten more years and do the same. Different situations, but did you have similar reactions?

Step Five

Then go back ten more years until you reach your earliest years. You may not have clear memories of when you were two or three years old. However, based on what you know of your family situation at the time, you may have a sense of what incidents impacted you. For example, your family may have moved, another child was born, or someone died. Perhaps another tragic situation occurred: mom was left alone to care for the children, dad left home to find a job, etc. You may have felt fear, anger, or bitterness in response to those events that repeated itself in situation after situation for each decade.

STEP SIX

After writing down what you remember, look over what you have written down. Do you see a pattern? Underline elements of that pattern.

STEP SEVEN

Sit with what you have observed. Allow yourself to experience the associated feelings, thoughts, and physical sensations. Be watchful and attentive, yet still and non-reactive. This may be difficult and uncomfortable at first, but it is important to acknowledge and to welcome this reality into your awareness. While these inner forces remain unconscious, they can powerfully affect you and influencing your decisions. When they have been made conscious through this attentive watchfulness, they begin to lose their power. As you sit without reacting to the forces that tug at your mind and heart, they will begin to subside.

When you have done this exercise at least once and identified a pattern, observe how it plays out in your day-to-day life. Bring the patterns you have identified to people you trust and see what they think. And finally, ask God to help you break out of the pattern you have discovered. God wants to set you free.

Chapter Three

God Wants to Establish Something New

The Parable of the Prodigal Son is a study in patterns. Both sons had a set way of relating to their father. The younger son always took charge of his future, without thinking about others. His pattern was to decide what he wanted, make his plans, and carry them out. He demanded his share of the inheritance and then went on to live a life of luxury, spending the money until he had wasted it all. Even when he ended up with nothing, he returned to his father with a plan: to join the hired hands on his father's farm and to work his way back into the family, paying back what he squandered.

The elder son, on the other hand, reacted angrily and complained when his father threw a party to celebrate his brother's return. He didn't trust his father's love for him, and he resented his younger brother's irresponsibility. The elder son's pattern was to play the obedient son, to exteriorly follow the rules, but only to get what was one day coming to him. He controlled his anger under perfect obedience.

The father's love stopped each boy in his tracks and gave them the opposite of what they expected. The younger son expected punishment from his father, who instead celebrated his return. The elder son expected strict justice for himself and for his brother, but his father called him to mercy by giving him mercy, too.

The father never withdrew his love from either son. He freely gave his younger son his inheritance. When the younger son walked into his father's life after months or years away, his father didn't ask him why he had returned. He didn't say, "Well, okay, you can come home, but don't expect. . . ." And to the older son he said, "All that is mine is yours!" (Lk 15:21). The father's love was not stingy or callous but absolutely generous, even lavish.

God surprises you with a welcome *beyond* your imaginings.

In thinking about the Parable of the Prodigal Son, we usually focus on the younger son's regrets. But the elder son also had many regrets. He was angry that the younger son would now live off of his own inheritance. Perhaps the older son regretted that he hadn't been honest and told his father that he did not feel appreciated.

The father could have had many regrets. He had permanently lost a lot of money when the younger son left. He also didn't have his younger son's assistance on the farm. His heart suffered because he didn't know where his son was. Yet the father continued to love. He was the only person in the story who did not demand that others meet his needs and desires. Instead, he simply loved others and gave himself away to them. The father is the only figure in the parable who loves unconditionally. His loving goodness amazes us. This love allowed the younger son to return and claim his place in the family.

Just as both the older and younger son must have been amazed when their father loved them unconditionally, Jake also was overwhelmed when God unexpectedly revealed his love: "You are standing on holy ground. Everywhere is holy ground. Everything is sacred." In that instant, Jake saw his situation with the eyes of his heart. He knew that all his regrets had become a window through which God's grace was shining on him. He had come face to face with God in the depths of his soul, and God's hospitable, welcoming love had surprised him. Jake was washed with the refreshing waters of the Father's mercy, and something new finally seemed possible. Of course, Jake's journey did not end when he heard God's voice that day. He still struggled with feelings of depression and guilt. But he had begun a journey with God toward self-acceptance.

When God surprises you with a welcome beyond your imaginings, you may feel confused. Like the prodigal son, you may think God expects you to wallow in regrets and self-pity. You may be surprised to find that upon seeing your regret-filled heart, God doesn't harshly chastise you but instead welcomes you. These sacred moments of true sight reveal the disparity between how you see yourself and how God sees you.

One day, God will surprise you just as he surprised Jake. God will help you to become comfortable with the positive and negative in your life, both the lights and the shadows. God will help you to be at peace with your journey of integration and transformation.

God wants to throw you a party.

He doesn't want to hear the story of who you think you are. He will interrupt you, as the father did in the parable, so you can hear God's story of who you are. Only that story matters.

Let the party begin!

Exercise
Look upon Yourself with Kindness

Let's pause here.

Have any bells gone off? Memories popped up? Realizations surprised you? Have you identified a pattern in your life that leads to regret?

Even if you haven't discovered anything, that's okay. This journey is not meant to be a goal-oriented race, speeding toward a destination. Absolute focus on results usually doesn't help a person's healing process. What does help is a spirit of gentleness, wonder, and trust.

This exercise will help you to relax, let go of any pressure you may feel, and begin to experience the Father's unconditional love.

STEP ONE

Reflect on your life and make a list of the things for which you feel regret.

STEP TWO

If there is anything for which you feel repentance, pray:

○   "Father, please forgive me for _____."

Step Three

Imagine the Father interrupting you and showing you his love, as in the parable. Accept the Father's love.

Step Four

Then say:

- ○ "Even though I have _____, the Father accepts me with compassion."
- ○ "Even though I have experienced _____, the Father looks upon me with kindness."
- ○ "Even if I did _____, God still loves me."

Step Five

After you have accepted God's love, try showing yourself the same unconditional love. Say to yourself:

- ○ "Even though I have _____, I accept myself with compassion."
- ○ "Even though I have experienced _____, I look upon myself with kindness."
- ○ "Even if _____, I completely love myself, my deepest self."

Step Six

As you remind yourself of God's never-ending love and show yourself kindness, the fearful, sinful, wounded aspects of who you are and all you have experienced will have the courage to come more strongly into your awareness. Show them the Father's mercy, the mercy you would show a small child who has the courage to tell you the truth about his or her hurts. Practice saying to this courageous yet vulnerable aspect of who you are, "You are part of me, and I claim you as my own."

Step Seven

What do you notice now about the way you are thinking, feeling, and expecting? Journal or write down what you are experiencing, or just sit in silence and accept it with gratitude.

Prayer Moment

You are not the runaway son or the elder son. You are you, with your own story. Have the courage to tell your story to your heavenly Father so he can show you how much he loves you.

Step One

Find a quiet place to sit and close your eyes.

Step Two

Imagine the Father in heaven looking at you. Receive his gaze. Listen to him say, "If you only knew how much I love you." Spend some time with your response to these words, whatever it is.

Step Three

Tell the Father about your life, your story, and your regrets. Hear him say, "Shh. Enough. Let me embrace you. Let me dance for joy that I have you back. I hope you never tear yourself away from my love again, but even if you should, I will still take you back. Again and again. Over and over. Because love can do nothing less."

STEP FOUR

Stay in this moment for as long as you can. Soak up the Father's love. Do you hear him saying anything that is for you alone to hear? These words are important to record somewhere so that you can return to them.

PART TWO

God's Second Promise to You

*Look at me, and you
will know who you are.*

When Jesus saw her, he called her over and said,
"Woman, you are set free from your ailment."

— Luke 13:12

*T*houghts are powerful. The concept you have of yourself is patched together from a lifetime of feelings, memories, impressions, fears, and sorrows. Your regrets and how you see yourself because of them can be a source of great pain. But as your heart is thrown wide open in agony, you will discover a treasure you never knew was there: the presence of God that grows stronger and stronger. When the Lord appears in your pain, and you look into his face, you will know who you really are. This part of the book will show you how to reject destructive thoughts and embrace your life as it really is so you can begin to live in the presence of God.

CHAPTER ONE

"Be freed from your disability."

The woman shuffled into the synagogue where the young Rabbi from Nazareth was speaking. As she moved around the edges of the crowd, hoping not to be seen, the woman could hear the conversations around her. A few comments were thrown her way, in pity or disgust. For the past eighteen years, all she could see when she walked around were the feet of those who filled the synagogue. Year after year, she had been unable to stand upright, bent over double. She had resigned herself to her place in the pecking order of her day. Her desires for wholeness, health, and freedom from anonymity and poverty had been dashed again and again. Others thought she was in the way—unimportant, unseen, unheard, and, indeed, unknown.

Suddenly, the woman noticed the feet around her backing away from her field of vision. A hush replaced the chatter that had surrounded her just a moment ago. Uncertain, she stood still long enough to hear the words floating above her, "Woman, come here."

A stab of fear made her almost crumble to the ground, but she caught herself and slowly followed the sound of the kind voice.

"Woman, come."

When she reached the place where she thought the voice had been coming from, there was only silence. She felt embarrassed. She couldn't see what was happening; she only knew she was standing before the person who spoke with unexpected tenderness. Hands, gentle yet firm, touched her, and a feeling like the crashing of waves swept over her.

"Woman, you are freed from your disability."

She felt a freshness and youthfulness she couldn't remember ever experiencing. Slowly, she began to lift herself, to straighten herself. First she saw the hands of the Rabbi who had spoken these words of healing to her. Then she did something she couldn't have done before. She looked straight into his face, the first face she had seen in many years. She shifted her weight as she looked around the silent synagogue. No face radiated such kindness as the face of Jesus did.

Suddenly the leader of the synagogue stood up and broke the silence. "Don't come here on the Sabbath to be healed. There are six days for work and those are the days to seek healing."

Jesus stepped between the woman and man speaking. "Wouldn't you untie your ox or your donkey from their stall and lead them out to water on the Sabbath?" The man looked down. Jesus continued, "Tell me! Don't you free your animals on the Sabbath so they can eat?"

The silence was deafening, and all the people in the crowd looked away from Jesus. The woman started to back away, seeking to disappear into the shadows. Jesus reached out his arm in her direction and asked, "If you would take care of the needs of your animals, how much more should I have freed this woman, this daughter of Abraham, from her bondage. For eighteen long years, Satan has kept her bound. Why can't she be freed on the Sabbath day?"

Daughter of Abraham! she repeated to herself. *Daughter of Abraham. No one even noticed me before. No one cared. No one, including me. But Jesus sees me not as a cripple, but as a member of the community.*

As the synagogue emptied out, Jesus looked at her with an encouraging smile. He gestured toward the entrance and they both walked into the future.

— Meditation based on Luke 13:10–17

Prayer Moment

(See page 15 for detailed instructions on how to pray with Scripture.)

The woman bent double, seeing only the ground, is an image of each of us. After the Fall, the human race suffered manifold illnesses, unable to find a remedy or cure. In the woman bent double, Jesus saw all of humanity bound captive by the devil. He saw fallen humanity, separated from God and unable to unite itself to him. Jesus saw our weakness and was filled with compassion.

Like all of fallen humanity, you too know what it is like to feel far from the warmth of the Father's tender gaze, afraid of his love, of the cost of entrusting yourself wholly to his dream for your life. Like the woman bent double, you are in some way living content or resigned to your illness.

Are you ready to break free?

STEP ONE

Imagine yourself as the woman bent double. Don't think about her, watch her, or pray about her. Instead, enter into her experience. *Feel* what she felt. Suffer her loneliness and sadness from within. See what she sees as she shuffles down the ancient dusty streets. What does she hear, touch, taste? How does she feel about herself? Does she hope for anything? Has she given up hope?

STEP TWO

Experience the woman's desperation on every level of your being; she couldn't find relief or a cure anywhere. What is she thinking? What is her attitude? How does she live with her illness? Has she become used to being sick? Adjusted her sight to the horizons of her illness? Is sickness her new health? Is sickness how she measured a good day?

STEP THREE

Merge with this woman, for she is *you* in some area of your life. What is it that *you* need to be freed from? What is it *you* haven't told a single soul, but carry locked away, hidden even from yourself? What is it that *you* desire?

As a member of the human race, you are also sick, spiritually ill, suffering from an illness that casts you into the darkness. You have made friends with something you regret. In some aspect of your life, you are resigned to being ill and expect nothing new, nothing more. You think, *This is just the way it is. I can't even begin to imagine anything different.*

STEP FOUR

Hear the words of Jesus said over *you*: "You are freed of your disability" (see Lk 13:12). What did the woman see when she looked into Jesus' face, the first face she had seen in almost twenty years? What did she see in his eyes? What do *you* see in his eyes? Joy? Excitement? Compassion? Do Jesus' eyes convey that you are the beloved of his Father? The work of his creative love?

What does Jesus want to say to you?

———◇—◇———

When we use our imagination to pray with Scripture, we can be profoundly moved by grace. We might notice new insights, new desires, or a shift that we can't quite explain or deny. What new insights do you notice? How is God moving your heart? What new perspective do you have on a situation in your life? How do you feel God calling you to respond differently to him or to others? How have you experienced God's love in a new way?

CHAPTER TWO

Get in Touch with Your Pain

Angie turned over in her bed and faced the wall. She was recovering from breast cancer treatment, but now her health was the least of her worries. Her heart sank as she thought of her two teenage girls. How could she tell them that their father wanted a divorce? "I haven't been happy for a long time," he had told her the night before. "I'm going to leave. You and the girls will be fine." Over and over again the words "will be fine" ricocheted around her mind. "Fine." She didn't feel fine. She didn't know what to do. She didn't know how she would make it on her own.

I met Angie for HeartWork sessions shortly after her husband asked for a divorce. As she told me her story I realized how alone she was. She had moved away from her family for the sake of her husband's education. She had no friends or family nearby. Her husband was leaving her for a student he had met while working on his doctorate. Angie had so many regrets. Over and over, she asked herself, "How could I have been so stupid to bring my girls here? Far away from my parents, with no support. How could I have done this?"

As we explored Angie feeling about herself in this situation, we noticed a pattern. For much of her life she had felt unworthy, powerless, and no good. She recounted a childhood memory when her father told her, "You can't do anything right," because she had earned two Bs on her report card. Her father had sent her to her room to study, while he took the rest of the family to the movies. The sense of isolation and worthlessness she felt in that moment had continued throughout her life and had eaten away at her self-confidence. Timid and fearful, she always felt as if she were waiting to discover again that she wasn't good enough, wasn't wanted.

Taking Thoughts Captive

When I first started paying attention to my thoughts, I couldn't believe how hateful I was to myself. If most of us paid attention to our thoughts and feelings, we would notice that much of what we think about ourselves is not kind. Our thoughts are often filled with judgment or even self-hate. The stories we tell ourselves, the stories through which we put ourselves down, are often tall tales. They are not based on facts. To get unstuck, we need to first separate ourselves from them.

During one session when we met, I led Angie through a very simple practice of prayer. After she became present to herself and aware of her breathing, I asked her to relax her body from head to toe. Quietly, she observed her thoughts. She noted her emotions. She noticed her judgments of herself, others, and situations.

"You are not your thoughts or your feelings," I told her. "You are more than these things. You *have* feelings. You *think* thoughts. You can observe your thoughts, but you can also detach yourself from them. You can be present to your thoughts but not captive, so that you may find serenity."

Saint Maximus and other Fathers of the Church tell us to plunge our mind into our hearts, to bury our thoughts in the name of Jesus, and to take our thoughts captive by attentiveness to the face of Jesus. So I taught Angie a simple prayer she could say quietly, each phrase on a breath, if she was feeling overwhelmed with negative thoughts: *Here–now–I'm yours–Jesus.*

During another session, I invited Angie to return to when she was a little girl left alone in her room to study, then to ask Jesus to be with her. I prayed quietly as she invited Jesus to come into her heart. Angie imagined Jesus in her room and she told him how angry, powerless, and unworthy she was feeling. I asked her just to watch how Jesus responded. After a while, I asked her what she saw Jesus doing. Angie wiped tears from her eyes and said, "Jesus sat down next to me and took out a chess board. I have always loved to play chess. He had all the time in the world just to play chess with me, to make me happy!" I asked Angie how she felt about what happened in her prayer. "I couldn't believe someone could love me. It felt warm. Beautiful."

Prayer experiences like this, just a simple encounter with God, can powerfully change the practical situations of our lives without any effort. Over the next few months, we began to explore Angie's prayer experience, to strengthen her roots in the ground of being discovered, shaped by, and protected in the hands of a loving God. Angie's husband didn't change his mind, but Angie began to find herself again, and that made all the difference.

The First Step Toward Healing

Once, I was helping with renovating an area of the convent where I live. We pulled up carpets, scraped up glue, stripped and waxed floors, and moved furniture. After a few days of hard work,

I wasn't able to sleep at all. I went to the living room one evening and started doing the simple breathing exercise outlined earlier. As I said, *Here—now—I'm yours—Jesus,* within seconds I noticed that my feet were screaming in pain. I looked at them and saw open blisters on the soles of my feet. No wonder I couldn't sleep! I soaked my feet, and soon my insomnia passed. This story is a simple illustration of what can happen to us when we are in spiritual or emotional pain and are not aware—or don't want to be aware.

If you find the *new,* then tomorrow will never be as yesterday.

Both the woman bent double and Angie were in pain. They had every reason to ignore what they felt in order to keep going. But getting in touch with our pain is the first step toward healing. In Angie's case, there was a lot going on interiorly that she needed to face first in order to find healing. She was scared, but she was also angry. Angie also felt guilty that she had agreed to move, a decision she now feared would negatively impact her daughters' lives. She felt deficient. Ugly. Loveless. Depressed. Lonely. I helped Angie to face how she was feeling—on all the levels—so that she could learn to let it be, to accept where she was, and to stop trying to escape it.

Getting in touch with our pain can be difficult. We often have uncomfortable feelings on every level of our being. When we become present to the here and now we suddenly touch what *is* here and now. Then we say OUCH! But the healing process begins at this moment, when we learn to develop a tender gaze toward ourselves in the reality of the present moment.

Like Angie, you may be living with pain as a result of not being able to forgive yourself. Maybe you just keep going, put on a smile, take care of others, and hold down a job, but inside you hurt. It is only natural that you try to escape what hurts you—either physically or emotionally. To protect yourself, you have closed the door to what you regret and pretend all is fine. The problem with this strategy, however, is that you live more and more in a reality that is a mental construct, and you distance yourself from the very things that can heal you. When you accept your pain, you will find the freedom to look at your life with new eyes. The situations that break your heart and tear you to pieces ask of you something new, and if you find the *new*, then tomorrow will never be as yesterday.

Embrace Your Life as It Is

Part of maturing is making peace with the life that is ours, past and present. If we can't forget the things we've done and instead continually think of our mistakes, or feel constant guilt, we cannot accept ourselves and all that our life has been—both the light and the shadows. Judgments, comparisons, labels, excuses, and analyses stand in the way of making peace with the life we have lived. Surrender is possible only when we live in the absolute immediacy of our experience without commentary and rejection.

At any given moment one thing, and one thing only, is happening. I'm sitting. I'm listening. I'm talking. I'm singing. I'm kneeling.

I'm folding my hands. I'm praying. I'm eating. My hands are in the sink. I'm washing dishes. Most of the time, we aren't attentive to the immediacy of the present experience. We are thinking of something else. We are commenting to ourselves on how much we like something, or how this is better than that, or we are asking ourselves why this person next to us is doing what she is doing. We replay the past and rehearse the future. We live in a world of our own creation and miss out on the beauty of God's world. We live in *God's* world when we are fully awake to what is currently unfolding, when we receive it silently, with curiosity and wonder. Full awareness includes opening ourselves to reality without judgment as to whether the present moment is pleasant or painful. Very few people take a moment to experience the present.

You can take a giant step toward letting go of your regrets by simply embracing each moment, as it is, with love. Each moment is allowed by a God who sustains you in existence, bends over your littleness, and requires nothing of you but surrender to his loving providence. You may not like what you feel or what see in yourself. Our concept of ourselves usually involves ideas of what we would rather be or who we think we should be. But God doesn't love the imaginary you. He loves the you he has created. Right now that includes the discomfort you may feel about yourself. Staying present to this discomfort is key to maturing in self-acceptance and to, one day, forgive yourself.

Exercise
Only This Moment Is Yours

Touching your history and accepting your reality takes courage. The past cannot be changed, no matter how much we may desire it. Trying to change or fix it is a trap. It means you want to be somewhere else, someone else. You may wish your life had been different. This may seem like a good thing. But in reality we reject ourselves when we want something that can never be real (but would be nice if it were).

God is here now, and with you *as you are*.

This exercise will help you to embrace your here-and-now experience.

STEP ONE

Start by simply breathing. Take a few deep breaths. You may not realize how shallow your breathing has become as you carry around your secret shame. Breathing can bring you home to body and soul, while shame causes you to disengage from yourself. What do you feel as you breathe? Breathe in. Breathe out. Focus on just breathing for about eight minutes.

STEP TWO

Take some time to be aware of your thoughts. What do you hear in the room around you? What are you thinking? Turning within, what do you hear? What do you see? What do you taste? Are your thoughts life-giving? Harsh? Fearful?

STEP THREE

In coordination with your breathing, say this simple reminder to yourself:

- ○ *I am here.*
- ○ *I am here now.*
- ○ *That is all.*
- ○ *I am here.*
- ○ *I am here now. That is all.*

STEP FOUR

Do you perceive any shift in your awareness? What are you feeling? Some people will feel a great inner peace. Others will experience an inner agitation or anxiety. Whatever you feel is fine. Consider writing down what you are experiencing or sharing it with another person if it is helpful.

Chapter Three

Jesus Sees Who You Really Are

The woman bent over double was an outcast. She was the woman no one cared about. The one no one knew what to do with. People talked over or around her, but rarely spoke to her. She had no hope for a cure. Everything she had tried had failed. Maybe she even thought she was a failure, that her life was wasted.

But when Jesus called the woman over, she straightened up at his word. Now, able to stand up, see, and return to the community, she regained her identity. She learned who she really was *directly* from Jesus. He bent over her in mercy because he loved her. He tenderly reached out to her because she was precious. His was the first face she saw and Jesus' eyes told her that he respected and loved her as she was.

When Jesus responded to the Pharisees who complained that he had cured someone on the Sabbath, he didn't refer to her as "this cripple," or "that woman." He called her "a daughter of Abraham" (Lk 13:16). He restored her to her place in salvation history, one of the children promised to the great patriarch

Abraham when God directed him to look at the sky and said, "I will make your offspring as numerous as the stars of heaven and as the sand that is on the seashore" (Gen 22:17).

In that moment, this daughter of Abraham discovered that all she had thought about herself had no truth in reality. Her self-concept, which had been created from patched-together fears, judgments, memories, and sorrows, was simply a product of her changing thoughts and emotions. Only in Jesus' face could the woman see who she truly was. Only in his love for her could she discover her life's value.

Similarly, for Angie the fearful prospect of divorce and of being alone initiated a spiral of negative worries and thoughts. *What will happen to the kids? Why didn't I see this coming? I'm not good enough for him. What should I have done better? What could have made a difference?* The onslaught of self-questioning and shame made Angie more and more depressed. She needed to get out from under the weight of her own idea of who she was and to hear from *Jesus* who she was. That is why we invited Jesus back into Angie's childhood memory of being left home alone. In that prayer, Angie spoke directly to Jesus about her pain, and he came into her heart precisely in the way that would make her feel most safe, known, and loved.

What about your life? Jesus wants to get personal in the same way with you. Give him the chance to tell you what he thinks about you. Speak directly to Jesus, tell him what you think about yourself as a result of the experiences in your life. When you do so, watch him. The eyes of your heart will not fool you. We may think God doesn't hear our prayers because we can't hear his voice, or he doesn't do what we ask. But if you simply watch him, Jesus will do the unexpected. He will surprise you with something beyond your imagination. When Jesus played chess with

Angie, this remarkably intimate gesture said more to her than if she had imagined Jesus saying, "I love you," or if she had read about God's love in a book.

Getting in touch with our anguish and telling Jesus about it helps us to enter the amazing mystery of God's love. Normally we fear the unknown depths of our sorrow and fear. We resist it. We turn in the other direction. We push it out of our sight. We pretend we are happy. We present ourselves to the world as strong and good. We refuse to face what we are feeling inside. This is a violent way to treat ourselves. How we suffer when we do it!

It is important to feel in a *positive* way our humanity that makes us suffer and breaks us to pieces. From every ending, a new beginning. Our humanness reveals to us that we are made for the Infinite. Nothing less than the Infinite can satisfy us. The pain we feel is the means of becoming aware of Jesus. It is the instrument through which Jesus makes himself present. For this reason, we must open ourselves to our pain and be acutely aware of how it reverberates in us on every level of our being: in our bodies, in our emotions, and in our thoughts.

A willingness to seek the complete meaning of what we feel is crucial to the healing process. For example, one day I was meeting in a coffee shop with two sisters. We were speaking about a project we all were working on. At one point, the other two sisters proceeded to divide the writing aspects of the project between themselves. It didn't occur to them that I could contribute. At least that was how I interpreted what happened. It was a small thing, so small I felt guilty that I felt it so deeply. But for some time, I had been noticing that others were being chosen for tasks, other projects I had worked on were rejected, and still others had failed. I was feeling very vulnerable already, so this small incident hurt me more deeply than it normally would have.

When we returned home, I took a walk in the backyard where I could be alone. I reminded myself that God was at work in all that was happening in my life. Yet it still hurt. As I looked across the new spring garden dotted with the bravest flowers beginning to poke above the soil, I began to cry. I embraced my sorrow and disappointment. From somewhere deep within, a courageous prayer came forth: *Jesus, take everything, everything, but give me yourself.*

In difficult situations like this, you can discover a quiet, strong, and often unaccessed place within you when you take the risk to open wide your anxious heart. What is that place? It is the hidden center of your being where the Trinity came to dwell in you at your Baptism. In this sacred sanctuary, Christ inspires and encourages you to choose what is true, good, and beautiful. The more you live in this quiet stillness, shielded from the chaos of your immediate reactions to situations, the more the graces of your Baptism can become active in your life.

Nicholas Cabasilas, fourteenth-century humanist, philosopher, theologian, and mystic, wrote of our Baptism:

> When we come up from the water, we bear the Savior upon our souls, on our heads, on our eyes, in our very inward parts, on all our members—Him who is pure from sin, free from all corruption, just as He was when He rose again and appeared to His disciples. . . . Thus we have been born; we have been stamped with Christ. . . . As He blends and mingles Himself with us throughout, He makes us His own body.[1]

The graces of your Baptism may seem mysterious, mystical, and not quite as real and effective as action, decision, opinion, or argument. But in reality, it is just the opposite. The graces of your

---

1. Nicholas Cabasilas, *The Life in Christ* (Yonkers: SVS Press, 1997), 62.

Baptism, strengthened and renewed through the sacrament of Confession, are the presence of God within you.

Find shelter from the storm of your regret and fear in the stillness of the sanctuary where God is active within you. A renewed humanity that is brave, tender, and real will blossom there. God doesn't cause the painful situations in your life, but as your heart is torn open wide in agony, you will discover a treasure you never knew was inside of you: the presence of God that grows stronger and stronger.

God is *active* within you.

Exercise
Meditation on a Grain of Sand

Our regrets can seem almost impossible to navigate. Painful situations and memories are often complex and confusing. Instead of trying to find your way through the labyrinths of pain, you can find more new freedom by accepting and embracing the present moment.

Step One

Close your eyes and picture yourself as a grain of sand on the seashore. Embrace the littleness and simplicity of the grain of sand.

What would it be like to be as simple and unpretentious as a grain of sand: small, insignificant, completely surrendered to the power of the wind and the sea? Spend some time imagining what that would be like. Be attentive only to your imagination and what you are experiencing, allow all else—negative thoughts, regrets, looking to the past or future—to wash away.

Step Two

Imagine yourself building a sand castle. In your bucket press into the sand the regrets that give you the most anguish. Keep adding to your sand castle until every one of your regrets is in some way represented.

Step Three

Now step away some distance, perhaps sit on a chair or on a rock. Watch the tide come in, closer and closer to your sand castle. Observe the water surround, cover, and then gradually wash the castle away. Rejoice as your regrets disappear under the gentle movement of the tide.

- ○ What would it be like to let go of your regrets?
- ○ What would it be like to drop the demands you are making of yourself?
- ○ What difference would this make in the way you feel about yourself? About others? About God?

Step Four

If it is helpful, write down or discuss with a friend or loved one how you felt in this exercise as you let go of the past and began to live in the present.

Prayer Moment

How you see yourself is not the truth. Only Jesus can tell you who you truly are. Give him the chance to reveal to you how he sees you.

STEP ONE

Take a moment to honor this place in your journey. Be still for a few moments, then bring to the surface some place in yourself where you are experiencing sorrow or regret. Picture in detail the situation that caused these feelings.

STEP TWO

Next, invite Jesus into your experience. Let Jesus see everything, simply, trustingly. With Jesus there, become aware of the whole texture of your experience. You may first notice a surface feeling, probably anger, grief, or fear. When you focus on this feeling, another feeling may make itself visible. If you see this new feeling or thought or reaction, show this to Jesus. When you focus on that new feeling, another feeling may make itself visible. With Jesus, unwrap all of the layers of how you are feeling about the situation that has caused you regret.

STEP THREE

Standing before all that you have uncovered, practice a tender loyalty to yourself in the presence of Jesus. Ask him to help you to relax. Try not to get lost in negative thoughts, just allow Jesus to look at what you are opening up before him. You may experience a surprising stillness. Say to yourself: "There is a place within me that desires something good, beautiful, and noble." That place within you will make itself known.

STEP FOUR

Now imagine Jesus sitting right next to you. Look directly in his face. What do you see? How does Jesus see you? How is this different from how you see yourself? Does Jesus want to tell you anything about who you are? What does he say to you?

STEP FIVE

Return to what Jesus has said to you over and over again. Make this sacred memory a new place for prayer, a reminder of how precious you are to God.

PART THREE

God's Third Promise to You

You see your failure,
I see your future.

Jesus said to her, "Everyone who drinks of this water will be thirsty again, but those who drink of the water that I will give them will never be thirsty."

— John 4:13–14

Regrets have a funny way of taking over your life. You spin the days, weeks, and years around the memories of your regrets. You may spend more time trying to fix or hide your regrets rather than just getting out of the way of what is happening now. But God isn't confined by what you think your life is or could become. No matter what you have done, Jesus says to you, "I have made you for more than this!" This part of the book shows you how to stop building your life around your regrets so that you might entrust the mystery of your future to the One who is, even now, creating your tomorrow.

Chapter One

"Those who drink . . . will never be thirsty."

A woman slowly meandered her way along a long dusty path to the village well. The noonday sun beat down on her head. Although most women usually did the heavy work of fetching water in the coolest hours of the day, she preferred avoiding others so she could be alone with her thoughts. She also wanted to avoid the comments and accusing glances of the other villagers.

The woman stopped and wiped her brow as she watched the heat dance off the rocks along the path. *Too bad it is such a long trip to the well,* she thought. A dull boredom had settled on her for several years. She struggled to do even the simplest daily tasks. Gradually her interest in life had dwindled. The life she had dreamed of for herself so long ago had never materialized. As she often did, she thought back to her first love; it had felt so new, so astonishing. *No, it's better not to remember. Just keep going,* she thought.

As she approached the well outside of town, she noticed a man sitting there alone. She looked at him warily. He hadn't withdrawn from the well as was customary to indicate it was safe to approach. She decided to go ahead and drop her bucket in the well. *I'll be out of here in just a minute*, she thought, silently addressing the unusual visitor. Heaving the bucket up, she placed it atop her head, ready to make the trek back to the village.

Suddenly the man spoke: "Give me a drink." The woman took a few steps and stopped. *Is he speaking to me?* The man's accent and mannerism betrayed he was a Jew.

"Please give me a drink."

The voice gently nudged her out of her safe cocoon of thoughts. Astounded, she turned and looked at him. For the man to even make eye contact with a woman in a public place was taboo, but it was unheard of for a Jew to drink water out of a Samaritan's unclean vessel.

"You're asking me for a drink? A woman? And a Samaritan?" she replied in amazement. But as she walked a few steps back toward the well where he sat, she found herself feeling warmed—almost welcomed—by his gaze. Something about his eyes entranced her. She gave him her full attention.

The man spoke again: "If you knew who I was and the gift I have for you, you would have asked *me* for a drink. I would have given you living water."

"How could I have asked *you* to provide me with a drink of water," the woman replied in disbelief. "You don't have a bucket here. This well is deep. Unless, of course, you think you're greater than our ancestor Jacob who gave us this well."

The man turned to look inside the well. Slowly he turned back to her and said, "This water is just like any other water. You drink it and you are thirsty again. I'm offering you another kind of water. Those who drink it will never be thirsty again. The water will become like a fountain of living water welling up within them."

Living water, she thought. *I wonder what that would be. If it means I don't have to walk out here every day, I'll take it.* She replied, "Sir, give me this water, so that I may never be thirsty or have to keep coming here to draw water."

The man looked at her gently. He leaned forward. The woman drew closer. She felt unsure, but a small hope bloomed in her heart that the man would give her something wonderful. Instead, she heard the words she most dreaded to hear:

"Go, call your husband, and come back."

The woman felt as though a door had banged shut within her spirit. *No! Who was this man?* she thought frantically. *What does he know about me to ask to do? Is he just another tongue-wagging bully like everyone else?* As her mind reeled she heard herself answer: "I have no husband." *Why did I even answer him?* She could have kicked herself.

"You are right. I know you don't have a husband. You have had five husbands, and the one you have now is not your husband."

He spoke gently, without shaming her or laughing at her. Just a simple statement of the truth. The man's respect for her pierced the dull scaffolding the woman had built up around her shaky insecurity. She felt it collapse. In one great, heaving sigh of relief, it fell at her feet—and his. The sword of his truthfulness had cut through the deadly lethargy of the buried lies she had been telling herself, and now she stood courageously before this tender man whose name she did not even know. At last. As her tears fell, the waters within began to bubble up and trickle into her inner desert. How her spirit craved this water!

As Jesus' apostles arrived at the well, the woman quickly gathered her jug of water and ran back to the village to tell everyone about this man who had seen everything about her without knowing her.

— Meditation based on John 4:5–30

Prayer Moment

(See page 15 for detailed instructions on how to pray with Scripture.)

The Samaritan woman's sins were no different from most of our sins. She was looking for love. But she looked in the wrong places. Jesus knew that, with his help, change for the Samaritan woman was possible. He offered the woman truth overflowing with mercy. Jesus knew that the power of his love would transform the woman's heart.

Like the Samaritan woman, perhaps you have looked for love in the wrong ways or in the wrong places. Or perhaps your love has been taken for granted, abused, or rejected. Thankfully, Jesus' love can heal your wounded heart.

Are you ready to accept his healing love?

STEP ONE

Imagine yourself as the woman of Samaria, a woman so hurt by the unforgiveness of others that she was completely unaware of her own need to forgive herself. Feel what she felt as her life unfolded in a way that left her disappointed and disillusioned. Never-ending gossip swirled around her wherever she went. The burdens and mistakes of her life had swallowed up the romantic desires and heartfelt enthusiasm of her youth.

Step Two

Experience on every level of your being how the Samaritan woman twisted and turned, trying to find a way to make sense of her life, to make it right, to see how it could be remedied. Imagine yourself as this woman, always replaying in her mind the moments of her life, looking for solutions. The complexity of her life had overwhelmed her, and she believed that nothing could be changed. Can you feel her pain?

Step Three

Imagine yourself as the woman before Jesus when he pointed out that she had five husbands. Observe how Jesus does not force you to acknowledge this reality or give a shame-filled explanation. Imagine when, like an arrow, the truth of Jesus' words pierced her heart, a heart that had suffered so long, drawing from your wounds the joy of repentance. Let yourself experience his love, this feeling of being wanted, known, seen, and desired. What does it feel like to be brought to life through Jesus' mercy?

Step Four

Merge your life with the Samaritan woman's experience of being found out in such a merciful, tender way. What secret are you hiding? What history do you feel can no longer be fixed in your life? Hear Jesus say your secret aloud. Stand before him as he looks at you and says, "I know. I know it all." Observe how Jesus does not demand that you grovel at his feet. Allow his loving,

truthful gaze to pierce your pain, forgive your sin, and set you free.
Jesus wants you to accept his offer of comfort and forgiveness.

STEP FIVE

Listen to Jesus tell you that he wants to become a living foun-
tain within you and to see your life overflow with grace and mercy.
He wants to send you running to the world to tell everyone that
God is merciful. Listen to Jesus say, "I want to see you happy."
When you stand before Jesus, what else does he say to you? Listen
to his words and observe his eyes and the way he relates to you.
Stand silently before him and accept his loving gaze.

What does Jesus see when he looks at you?

———◇◇———

When we use our imagination to pray with Scripture, we can
be profoundly moved by grace. We might notice new insights, new
desires, or a shift that we can't quite explain or deny. What new
insights do you notice? How is God moving your heart? What
new perspective do you have on a situation in your life? How do
you feel God calling you to respond differently to him or to others? How have you experienced God's love in a new way?

Chapter Two

Stop Building Your Life
Around Regrets

As Bill drove home one night from an AA meeting, rain pounded his car amid peals of thunder. The wipers bounced across his windshield, sending rain drops dancing. "I should have changed the wipers a long time ago," he muttered to himself, straining forward to see as he drove. His thoughts drifted to last year. *Last year.* It seemed so long ago. His business had failed and for months he had lived in his car, depressed, drinking, and wasting his life away.

Bill slowed down as he approached an intersection. Ignoring the stop sign, he turned right at the corner without seeing that a pedestrian had just stepped off the curb. Then he heard it. A thud. Everything happened in slow motion. As he slammed on the brakes, he saw someone roll across the hood of his car. His life flashed before him; all he had done, all he had experienced, all the people he had hurt, and all who had hurt him. Then, a voice spoke to him, whether in his heart or aloud, he didn't know and it didn't matter: "I have made you for more than this."

The sound of the rain beating on the windshield forced Bill back to the present. He stopped his car and jumped out. A woman in her twenties was lying on the ground. As a passerby called the police, Bill knelt down and covered the young woman with his coat. When help arrived, Bill watched as an ambulance whisked her away. Fortunately, the woman would be released from the hospital that night with only minor injuries. And, thankfully, Bill hadn't been drinking.

Sometimes powerful words from God engrave themselves on our spirits and can refashion a person's mind, will, and heart. Since that dark, rainy night, God's words had soaked into Bill's spirit. Many years later when Bill and I met for spiritual direction, we explored what had happened that fateful evening. The words *"You are meant for more than this"* had stuck with Bill since that night. Though Bill had turned the words over in his mind many times, he was not sure what they meant. He had no doubt that the words came from God, but there were many possible meanings. Did they mean that he should do something? Did God have a plan that Bill was supposed to figure out? Bill considered several possibilities, but they all seemed inadequate. After listening to Bill's understanding of those words since that night, I decided to share with him a paragraph from Jean-Pierre de Caussade, one of my favorite spiritual authors:

> [God] speaks while acting, for in God, to speak and to do what he wants are the same. Therefore, it is necessary to stop from time to time to make space for the impressions that God wants to imprint on our hearts and wills, which in an incomprehensible way he moves, turns, and fashions as he wishes, as long as no obstacle at all is found, much more easily than the most skillful

craftsman would know how to mold a piece of soft wax as he wishes.[2]

Bill and I decided to make just such a space for God to work. We sought to welcome and cherish the impressions that God had been imprinting on his heart.

I asked Bill to think back and relive the accident and the moment when he had heard the words: *"I have made you for more than this."* I invited him to close his eyes, go within himself, and to touch the ways that those words had moved him affectively when he had first heard them. As he returned to that moment, he realized that he had immediately felt excitement. For the first time in ages, Bill had felt hope and had seen the possibility of something new. He had felt as if he were being let out of a box that long had confined him. For many sessions Bill and I explored the impact of God's words on his soul. Whenever Bill began to speak about ideas or resolutions, I gently stopped him, and we returned to his work of the heart. I helped Bill to learn to practice passive receptivity to the Divine Craftsman who was molding him according to his own divine plans and re-creating him according to the divine dream for his life.

Bill and I met often, and for both of us it was time well-invested. Eventually, after he started focusing on getting out of the way instead of figuring out the way, God surprised Bill by sending him inspirations. They were so foreign to his way of thinking that Bill knew they had come from the same God who had spoken to him on that rainy night. God's words strongly

---

2. Jean Pierre de Caussade, S.J., *A Treatise on Prayer from the Heart: A Christian Mystical Tradition Recovered for All*, trans. Robert M. McKeon (Chesnut Hill: Institute of Jesuit Sources, 1998), 106.

impacted Bill the night he heard them, but the more he prayer-fully tasted those words and relished them over time, the more he could embrace the words of the psalmist, "Taste and see the goodness of the LORD" (Ps 34:8). Bill began to see the goodness of the future opening up before him.

We are greater than our regrets.

Bill's story is similar to that of the Samaritan woman. Both Bill and the woman quietly carried a dark sorrow within them. Both were burdened by failure, disappointment, and broken hearts. Both had unconsciously built their lives around their regrets, set-tling for what ultimately could bring them only sorrow. Their regrets and secrets had become a barrier to accepting God's love.

The Samaritan woman was disconnected from herself and oth-ers, trapped in a lifetime of mental categories and suspicion. She clearly did not trust Jesus at first. Though she had God in front of her, she remained in her own world, disconnected and apart from Jesus. Perhaps she expected Jesus to reject her as others had, or as she had rejected herself. Jesus, seeing her distrust, moved to estab-lish trust with her by asking for a drink. The woman still responded with distrust, however, asking him bluntly why he was talking to her, a woman and a Samaritan. Then, when Jesus promised the woman living water, she immediately thought about the practical benefits to fetching water without walking to the well. But Jesus patiently nudges her step by step away from her usual manner of thinking, and he invites the woman to trust in God and the world of "spirit and truth" (see Jn 4:24).

When Jesus addressed the Samaritan woman, I imagine he stood up as he spoke, excited to offer her living water. Perhaps Jesus was filled with joy at the thought that this lonely woman might accept his offer of divine love to become whole again. Though the woman was embarrassed by her failure and rejected by others because of her past, Jesus saw only her future. When we are seen, known, and heard by someone else, we discover that we are greater than our regrets and the way we've built our life around them.

Though Jesus approached the Samaritan woman and Bill in different ways, he invited them out of their prisons. He gave them room to breathe in the possibility that they were made for more. He didn't add to their self-blame with accusations. He knew they were already filled with regret and self-hate. Instead, he showed them that he believed in them and that they were worthy of his truthful love and strong enough to follow him on his way. Bill and the woman could forgive themselves because they knew that they had already been forgiven. Their desire to live was awakened by Jesus' desire that they leave behind their regrets and start to live fully.

God created the human heart to be like a large box vast enough to hold God himself. When we hate ourselves for what we've done or who we think we are, our hearts become smaller and smaller until our spirits have no more room to breathe. Sometimes we don't think we can bring our shame into the open before God. Perhaps you believe that God won't forgive you. You hide from God just as you hide from others when you are afraid to reveal your true self. At the root of this unhealthy behavior is the reality that you have rejected yourself. Do you love yourself in all your vulnerability and imperfection? When we refuse to allow ourselves to be held by God in the midst of our struggles, we deprive ourselves of God's tenderness toward us. When we lose ourselves in our regret, we lose sight of God, for whom our hearts were made.

God is not repelled or dismayed by your attempts to hide from him. He has his ways to reach you, as we saw with Bill and the Samaritan woman—marvelous, surprising ways. No matter what

God needs to do to reach out to you, the Lord will constantly try to help you to leave behind your regrets so that you can walk into your future.

Let go of secrets.

When we are living with a past haunted by regrets, we believe the lie that others are good and we are not. We may feel that we are unlovable, worthless, and insignificant. We avoid our inner desert because we fear being alone with our self-hate. So, we fill our lives with oases of success, happiness, or pleasure. We do anything we can to mask the emptiness, barrenness, and lifelessness. The only way to integrate our lives is through the merciful sword of truth. We shake with fear at being discovered for who we truly are until that sword is plunged into our souls.

Trust the God who sees your *future.*

Many of us excel at putting up a facade to protect ourselves. We embrace our pretenses, defenses, games, ploys, or idealized self-images as though they were real. We convince others and even ourselves that they *are* real. But if we look closely at the masks we wear, we discover they often project the opposite of the secret we seek to cover up. For example, if my secret is that I am unable to accept my own hostility toward others, I might create a mask that is sweet and kind. I may fool others for a while, I may even fool myself, but eventually the deception ends up bankrupting me. In time, my bitterness and hostility will come out in public, in a way I can't hide.

If my secret is that I regret having missed opportunities for advancement, I might cover my anger with a passive meekness. But beneath my humble words, a raging inner victim resents that others have what I don't. Or perhaps my secret is that I have seriously injured a relationship by something I did—maybe I had an affair, stole from someone, or lied. I may cover my guilt by denying that I did anything wrong or had any part in injuring another. I blame someone else. But once I have the courage of truth, I stop denying that what I did was truly wrong. I accept my part in the situation, and admit my fault. I accept that something needs to be confessed.

Secrets can distort our entire lives without our being completely aware of it. Often a part of our psyche tries to hide the truth, but secrets can cause emotional and physical illness until they are faced, admitted, and, when necessary, repented of. So take the courageous step to admit and repent of your secrets. Only an interest in the truth that is stronger than your interest in feeling good about yourself will unbind your heart and free you. Commitment to the truth enables you to show absolute respect to the present moment in all its joy or pain, trusting it to unfold in God's timing, not your own. The more open you are to your experiences as they come, and the more time and space you give yourself to live through what is happening without being pushed, hurried, or judged, the more you will discover the truth about yourself.

"You were made for more than this."

Those words caught Bill's attention, and he took them seriously. He stood watch over the woman he had hit with his car, shielding her from the rain, taking responsibility for the accident. To be fully in the present, fully in the moment, fully in the body, is to be fully in love with the truth of what God is doing in each moment. To love each moment with all that it brings is to trust the God who sees your future and who reaches out to you now.

Exercise
Live Beyond Secrets and Regrets

We all wear masks to protect ourselves. They help us to hide behind our secrets and regrets. But the winter of your pretense holds the promise of a new spring. Somewhere within you is the spontaneous, new, honest unfolding of your authentic self. It already exists; you just need to give up the masks you wear and live according to your true self.

This exercise will help you to descend into a space of simple knowing, where you can relax and rest, still, waiting, perceptive, peaceful. In this place of presence, you can let everything be. You can be a contemplative within the now, and walk forward into the future with God.

STEP ONE

Ask the Holy Spirit for the grace to see one of the images you hide behind and project into the world, trying to convince yourself and others of its genuineness. These masks may cover up regrets you feel or secrets you are trying to hide. They will appear to be positive, even if you are projecting a negative image, such as the image of a victim.

STEP TWO

Look closely at the image or facade that has come to your mind. You will see that it is not what you pretend it to be. Is there a secret that the facade is covering? Sit with this question for a while, perhaps in front of Jesus at the well as in the story of the Samaritan Woman, or in a favorite place of rest, or a sanctuary. Allow yourself to grow in deeper self-awareness. Wearing masks is a game we play, but it can cause harm.

STEP THREE

Consider the strength of the mask you are wearing and how much you feel you need them to protect yourself. Drop down deeper than your mask, which isn't you. It is a layer, a shell, covering the deepest core of your being, which is always beautiful and held in the hands of a God who creates only beautiful things. Observe the attachment you may have to this facade or mask, and go deeper. Let the attachment go.

STEP FOUR

Observe the reasons you use to keep this mask in place, and drop down. Observe any resistance or defensiveness you have to this process, and try to let that go. Continue to be aware of your thoughts, feelings, and reactions until you recall whatever experience you had that led you to use your facade. Refuse to possess it or attach yourself to it. Simply observe. Remain open, trembling but welcoming, waiting, ready to receive. Ask yourself:

○ What am I gaining by keeping up a facade?

○ Who is being affected by this role or game I am playing?

○ What secrets am I trying to hide?

STEP FIVE

State clearly to yourself how you have been hurt by living out of this false, idealized self-image. When you realize what those games have cost you and others, then you can decide to act differently. Ask yourself: How can I live without pretense and from a deeper truth? Write your answer in a journal if it is helpful.

God's Loving Embrace
Reveals Your Future

Both Bill and the Samaritan woman were searching for someone who could look beyond their past and see who they were really
made to be. Everyone wants to be loved, to know themselves as
loveable, and to receive unconditional love. Jesus is the One who
will understand and love us unconditionally. The imaginative
meditation on the Samaritan woman wasn't just a prayerful explo-
ration of something that happened to someone else. It wasn't a
fantasy. It wasn't a desperate wish that the same would happen to
you. The story, as it is related in the Gospel of John, tells you something about the way Jesus loves *you*. Christ offered the woman of
Samaria living water that would well up within her to eternal life.
In our Baptism, we have received the Living Water that washes and
prepares us for the life to come, that unites us to God.

Union with God is where we find our true identity in Christ.
Jesus says in the Gospel of John, "I am the vine, you are the
branches" (15:5). I often refer to this image of the vine and the
branches because it helps me to understand how God wants me to

relate to him. This image helps us all to understand how we can find happiness in God. If you visited a vineyard, the owner wouldn't say, "I have 35 vines, 400,000 branches, and 700,000 grapes." He speaks only of the vine. He would not mention all the parts of the vine because they all belong to the vine and draw life from the sap of the vine. The branches live in complete dependence on the life and health of the vine. Through our Baptism, we are called to live a similar reality.

We also truly belong to and are living members of Jesus (see 1 Cor 12). This is who we really are. When God told Bill that he was "made for more than this," he was telling Bill who he was. And God tells you the same thing. You are not a person who makes poor decisions or who struggles with this particular sin, or who ruined an opportunity, or who can't escape the trap of a physical challenge or emotional vulnerability, or who hurt another person. You may have *done* those things or *borne* those struggles, but they do not define who you *are*. The branch may be weak or diseased, but it remains part of the vine. And even if a branch has been cut off the vine, it can still be grafted back on. The resources of health that belong to the vine are passed to the branches most in need. When God sees your future, he sees you grafted onto him, living in peace and harmony with him.

Truth and Sacred Repentance

In the struggle to forgive ourselves we face the single greatest challenge: to stand in the truth of what we have done *and* in the truth that Christ invites us to close and intimate relationship with him. Jesus helped the Samaritan woman to accept the truth about her past so that she could walk into the future with him without her regrets. Similarly, when the early Christians in Corinth sinned,

Paul spoke truthfully about what they had done, but he also spoke the truth to them about who they were.

In his first letter to the Church in Corinth, Paul chastises the community for a flagrant sin in their midst: a man was sleeping with his father's wife (see 1 Cor 5:1). Paul directed the people to put this man out of the community in order that he might repent and return. Then Paul tells them the unexpected reason why this is important. He asks the people, "Do you know that a little yeast leavens the whole batch of dough?" (5:6). In other words, Paul points to how one person's actions can affect the entire Church's relationship with Christ. The reason sin was unacceptable for Paul was because it negatively impacts our relationship with God and identity in Christ. All sin, including sexual immorality, is a lapse in relationship, a painful wrenching of ourselves away from Christ, who loved us and died for us, who bought us with the high price of his death on the cross.

When I lead people through the journey you have been experiencing in this book, I often find that at a certain moment—a sacred moment—something wells up deep within a soul: repentance. Your regrets may be a mixture of things you have done, sins you have committed, and things that have happened to you. But all of us have done things we look back on with regret. In this journey of life, we experience regret around things we could have done differently, ways we have hurt others, words or actions we can never take back, and relationships that have ended. As you explore your regrets, do not feel surprised if you begin to feel the bubbling waters of a cleansing sorrow that are as different from burning shame as day is from night. This sorrow is pure gift, but we can ask God for this spiritual sensitivity.

Repentance is a step into the mystery of our salvation. It does not always feel good, but it ultimately leads us to wholeness and healing. Our human nature is frail, and we know from experience that we are dust, weak, and prone to sinful passions and desires, even when we know better. But God himself took up our struggle as his own. Christ came, as Healer and Savior, to heal the sickness of our human nature. When Christ was conceived in Mary's womb, he received from her his human nature. God became incarnate. In Christ the Word, his human nature was united to the divine nature in the unity of the second Person of the Trinity. Because he is divine, Jesus exalts our human nature and transforms it. Jesus became man, journeyed to Calvary, and rose from the dead so that we might become partakers of his divinity through faith and Baptism (see 2 Pt 1:4). By dying on the cross, Jesus took our sins upon himself, and by his resurrection he clothes us anew in the garments of his glory.

God's Presence Breaking Through

God broke into Bill's life when he said to him on that dark, rainy night: *"You were meant for more than this."* The Samaritan woman experienced God breaking through the pain and shame of her life when Jesus looked into her eyes and told her he could give her living water. The truth is that the eternal God breaks into our life all the time. God wants to give us the many graces available through the death and resurrection of Jesus Christ.

Perhaps you can think of a moment in your life when you felt God breaking through. Maybe you experienced a powerful realization as you struggled in prayer, or you felt an inner peace at the sight of a sunset. Perhaps an unexpected movement toward generosity arose when otherwise you might have been stingier with your time or treasure. Or maybe you felt a moment of joy when you realized God's fidelity. One or two profoundly moving experiences of God's mercy or closeness may already define your life, but you can learn to discover the wonder present in every day.

God is present to you in the past, present, and future. For God, all is the same because God is outside of time. As the author of Ecclesiastes writes,

> I know that whatever God does endures forever; nothing can be added to it, nor anything taken from it; God has done this, so that all should stand in awe before him. That which is, already has been; that which is to be, already is; and God seeks out what has gone by. (3:14–15)

If you can stay before this mystery and simply take it in, you will experience the presence of God who envelops you wherever you go. God's nearness will energize your soul and fill you with flashes of delight. As you grow in a sense of amazement at how God can be and how he is present in the tiniest details of your life, you will become more courageous and trusting. God wants to constantly reveal to you his unending tenderness. Have faith and believe that God can break the chains that hold you back.

Exercise
Discover the Joy of Repentance

Imagine you are destitute and need an operation to save your life. How would you feel if someone paid for it? What if that person did more than pay your hospital bill? What if he took you into his house while you recovered? And what if you also found out that this benefactor had decided to adopt you into his family and bequeath to you his entire fortune? You probably would have no words to express your gratitude in the face of such generosity.

This is what Christ has done for us.

STEP ONE

Imagine you are standing before the throne of God in heaven or side by side with Jesus. See the angels gathering around you in welcome, and the saints encouraging you. Know that you—a child of God, a brother or sister of Jesus Christ, sanctified by the Holy Spirit—belong in this place of light and glory and beauty. Feel your awe melt into love, an incredible humble gratitude in response to what you have been given.

God is *present* to you
in the past, present, and future . . .

STEP TWO

Take a moment to consider God's immense love for you. As you receive God's immense love, you may feel a mixture of emotions. Perhaps God's love has brought to light an awareness of emptiness, a spiritual poverty, moral illness, mediocrity, or wasted opportunities you have experienced in your life. If this should happen, it is a great grace. This awareness will spur you on to loving repentance. The greater your love for Jesus, the sweeter and more genuine your repentance.

You may wish to pray with these or similar words:

Yes, Lord, I choose you. I repent of betraying you, of choosing safety, security, material possessions, other people, and the world's success as my primary source of happiness over you. I realize what I have lost: You. Face to face with your love for me, I cannot avoid being aware of what I've lost.

STEP THREE

Do you feel Jesus inviting you to leave behind anything in order to enter more decisively into the reality of your Christian life? Take a moment to write down some behaviors that come to your mind that you feel inspired to ask for God's grace to change. As you look at your list, ask the Holy Spirit to help you to understand how these things have impacted your relationship with God. Does anything in particular move you to feel a tremendous sorrow that bubbles up from an experience of love? Do they move you to tears, at least spiritually? Which of them drive you into Jesus' arms?

STEP FOUR

Ask Jesus what you should do with this gift of repentance he has given you. Do not leave your prayer until you have a concrete and doable list of ways you feel called to express the joy of repentance that you have received.

Here is a list of possibilities:

- ○ the Sacrament of Penance;
- ○ an apology;
- ○ restitution;
- ○ assuming responsibility;
- ○ prayer and participation in Mass;
- ○ making a commitment;

○ almsgiving;

○ lifestyle changes.

Write down just one or two things that you feel inspired to do.

STEP FIVE

As you close this time of prayer, imagine yourself standing beneath the cross. You may feel inspired to write a prayer to Jesus that clearly states your resolution. Offer Jesus your plan and ask him for help. Put this prayer in a place where you can read it every day while you take the necessary steps to carry it out.

Prayer Moment

God is present to you now, in your past, and in your future. He is present in every moment of your life. Ask God to give you eyes of wonder so that you can see his presence.

STEP ONE

Take a moment to honor this place in your journey. Recollect yourself and sit for a while in stillness until your thoughts have ceased racing through your mind.

STEP TWO

Then, look through the events of today or the past week. Look for a time in which you experienced God breaking into your life. Where have you recognized God's presence? When have you noticed a flash of eternity amidst everyday life? What has deeply and unexpectedly moved you? What have you observed within you that seemed impossible without the grace of God? How have you sensed the presence of the eternal in an event that was unexplainable or surprising?

STEP THREE

When you have thought of an event, write down enough details to begin to fully appreciate the experience. How did the event unfold? Who was involved? How did you react emotionally? If you feel you responded well, what effect did that have on you and others? If you did not respond well, what accounts for that difference?

STEP FOUR

As you reflect upon the situation, close your eyes and imagine yourself back in that moment. Ask God to help you to recapture the sense of mystery and wonder at the movement of the divine in your daily life. Taste the experience again and live in it for a while.

Allow the Lord's love to embrace you. He sees you; he sees your future.

Rest in this loving presence.

PART FOUR

God's Fourth Promise to You

My light will radiate from you for all the world to see.

[Jesus] said to Simon, "Do you see this woman? I entered your house; you gave me no water for my feet, but she has bathed my feet with her tears and dried them with her hair."

— Luke 7:44

No path leads directly through darkness to dawn. When it comes to regrets, you may want to forget what you've done, how you've been hurt, choices you've made, or who you've injured. But often you can't. However, as your relationship with God grows stronger, you will discover that you are always in contact with God's love, a love more powerful than your regrets. This part of the book will help you to encounter God's mercy and to discover that your pain can be healed in the light of God.

CHAPTER ONE

"Go in peace."

The woman entered the house and tried to stay out of sight, huddled in the shadows. Everyone was awaiting the young Rabbi who had been invited to dinner at the house of Simon the Pharisee. The woman was absorbed in her thoughts and memories when she noticed one of the Pharisees glancing her way, as though trying to remember where he had seen her before.

Before, she thought.

Her past was no secret. She wished she could take a cloth and wipe it all away; completely remove her past from the memory of everyone who had known her. What once made her happy had turned to ashes. Now something within her yearned for more. For some time, whenever she had a chance, she had been listening to Jesus as he preached to the crowds. She felt something deep within her whenever she was in his presence; a light within her seemed to grow and make the darkness flee.

Finally, Jesus entered the room and the chatter ended. All eyes turned toward him. Nobody made a move or broke the deafening silence. Startled, the woman looked around. No one was showing Jesus any of the customary hospitality. No kiss of greeting. No washing of the hands and feet. No welcome of respect. Something was wrong. She couldn't understand. *How could they treat Jesus this way?* she wondered.

Jesus stopped, seeming to sense that there was more to this dinner than he had been told. Simon, flanked on each side by a group of Pharisees, was watching intently as Jesus looked around the room. Slowly, Jesus' open gaze rested on each face, moving from person to person, as if he were searching for someone he knew. The woman held her breath. *Will he remember me?* she thought. *I was just part of the crowds, one of the many who were being touched and transformed by his healing words. Why would I be special to him?* When she had listened to Jesus preach, the woman had experienced such hope, such promise, the sense that no matter what she had done, Jesus could and would help her make it right. She had come here because she felt that. But now, in the darkened room of Simon's house, she trembled.

What if he just passes over me? What if he doesn't care? The thought pierced her heart.

The woman held her breath as his eyes fell upon her face from across the room. Jesus' gaze rested on her for a moment that stretched into an eternity. And then, slowly, a smile spread across his face, a smile as beautiful as the sunrise. *He knows me,* her heart sang. And in that moment she felt the mercy of his eyes penetrating her heart, and she knew that he knew all about her, every last detail, *and still there was no doubt that he accepted her with loving mercy.*

Simon gestured to a table, and Jesus turned away. The woman felt so overcome with joy that she dropped to her knees. *I have been spiritually cleansed, at last!* she thought. Tears began to fall. *Thank you, God.* Then, an idea came to her. *No one washed Jesus' feet when he entered, but I can wash his feet with the only thing I have, my tears. I can serve Jesus in this small way.* She moved through the crowd until she reached him. Her tears—of love, sorrow, gratitude, and awe—fell quickly and covered Jesus' feet. "You see, Simon," she heard Jesus say, "the one who is forgiven much will love much, as this woman here. The one who thinks they have little for which they need to be forgiven will have little love."

The woman glanced up and saw Jesus looking at her. His gaze was one of gentle kindness and joy. Then he said, "Your faith has saved you, go in peace." The woman realized at that moment that she had encountered perfect mercy. Jesus had seen not who she was but who she could be. She knew then that her past was gone. Only her new identity existed in his eyes. From now on she was the woman who was the work of his hands, the gift of his divine love, with a future built only and forever on his love. Jesus, the Rabbi from Nazareth, had seen her truly. He had seen her heart's yearning, her desire to be freed from the chains that had enslaved her, from the power of the Evil One. Hers had been a lifetime of ugliness, hurt, self-hate. A life filled with rolling dark clouds, never a promise of sunlight. Her flowering hopes had always been crushed.

But it was now all over! Finished at last!

She had encountered mercy.

— *Meditation based on Luke 7:36–50*

Prayer Moment

(See page 15 for detailed instructions on how to pray with Scripture.)

The woman at the dinner party had a past that weighed heavily on her heart. Her heart was full of regret, missed opportunities, and embarrassing failures. But Jesus' heart was full of love for this woman. He desired to free her from the darkness of her regret so she could walk joyfully into his light.

You also may be held captive by the darkness of the past. Perhaps your days and nights are full of memories and reminders of the past, of your failures, of your deepest pains. Jesus invites you to look at him and find the light of his love. Experience your past brushed over with the radiant colors of a divine Artist, reframing the terror and the brokenness of your regrets through the mystery of his mercy.

STEP ONE

Imagine yourself as the woman who is waiting in the Pharisee's house for Jesus. Enter into her experience, the anxiety she feels as she waits for Jesus. The fear she must have felt when others looked at her and remembered her past. How does she feel about herself? What does she hope to see? Why has she decided to come to this house?

STEP TWO

Merge with the woman and wait as Jesus looks from face to face. When Jesus looks straight at you, allow yourself to be seen by him. Let his merciful gaze wash away a lifetime of regrets. Stay for some time just allowing Jesus to look upon you with his love. You could even stay for 20 or 30 minutes, simply allowing Jesus to look into your heart. Notice what you feel with his gaze upon you.

Step Three

Pray a silent prayer of joy from your heart straight to the heart of Jesus: "You remembered me and you love me! Jesus, I can't believe that you remembered me and that you love me!" What does Jesus say to you? Take some time to notice, to truly notice, not just details and facts, but also the movements of your soul as you listen to his answer, as his mercy washes over you. You may want to write these words down and read them after you receive the Eucharist or after the sacrament of Confession.

Step Four

Jesus saw the woman in the Pharisee's house in all her woundedness and sorrow, and he still accepted her. Her heart overflowing with gratitude, she decided to show her love for Jesus by washing his feet. How do you feel called to show your love to Jesus? Imagine yourself doing this or write down something that you plan to do in the future.

When we use our imagination to pray with Scripture, we can be profoundly moved by grace. We might notice new insights, new desires, or a shift that we can't quite explain or deny. What new insights do you notice? How is God moving your heart? What new perspective do you have on a situation in your life? How do you feel God calling you to respond differently to him or to others? How have you experienced God's love in a new way?

CHAPTER TWO

Encounter God's Mercy

I was standing nervously in the front of the conference room when a woman in her mid-forties, dressed in faded jeans and a wrinkled blouse, quietly took her seat. I was leading a weekend retreat for the first time for people suffering from depression. The woman, whose name I later learned was Bethany, caught my eye then looked away. She loudly greeted the other people filling the room, but a quiet sadness enveloped her, despite her gregariousness. At the end of my opening talk, I told the attendees that I would make myself available that evening to speak with anyone who wished to meet.

Some time after dinner Bethany knocked on the door. "I'm an alcoholic," she informed me bluntly as soon as we sat down. "I can't hold a job. So I spend most of my time going from one AA meeting to another. I know where all of them are held and I go with friends who have cars." She paused and looked at me cautiously, then said, "Do you think God hates me because I don't have a job?"

The question caught me off guard. "It sounds like there is a lot of suffering in your life," I ventured. Bethany looked long and hard at me, as if trying to make up her mind whether I was someone she could trust with her story. Leaning forward I added, "I don't think God hates anyone."

My response seemed to put Bethany at ease. She began to speak more freely, "You see, Sister, I haven't seen my children in years." Her eyes filled with tears. Gradually, she shared her story in fits and starts, interrupted by heartrending sobs. Before she was eighteen, Bethany had given birth to two boys and a girl. "And I haven't seen any of them," she said, her head in her hands. "They wouldn't let me see them even once. My parents decided I couldn't take care of them and we gave them up for adoption. But they wouldn't let me hold them, not even one time," she cried. Catching her breath, she said through sobs, "I've never . . . held . . . my . . . babies! I don't even know where they are. Or if they are okay."

Bethany told me how she had turned to alcohol to take the edge off the pain. She also buried her sorrow in food. Now she feared that her life was so badly messed up that she could never climb out of the hole she had dug for herself. When Bethany finished telling me her story, I waited for her tears to subside. I asked her if she would be open to meeting the next morning to pray together. She agreed.

After a good night's rest, Bethany was eager and ready for the guided prayer I had proposed. I explained to her that we would imagine how Jesus was present to bless her and her children at the moments when she gave birth. We began by quieting ourselves for prayer. I asked her to remember a beautiful place she had seen or visited. Bethany imagined herself deep in a quiet forest where she felt safe. She sat in a clearing on a fallen tree trunk as above her tree branches waved in the wind. She sat surrounded by sunlight playing hide and seek with the shadows.

I asked Bethany to imagine Jesus sitting next to her on the log. I encouraged her to share with Jesus what she had told me the night before. I waited until she seemed ready. Then I told her that for God all time is present. God doesn't experience past, present, and future as we do. So we can bring the past to Jesus now and he can provide for us what we needed then, and it can truly heal the pain of the past. I guided her to choose the birth of one of her children as the subject of our prayer. She chose her firstborn. Then I asked her to walk with Jesus through the forest into the hospital room where she had given birth to her eldest child. Bethany saw herself on the bed, ready to give birth. She remembered the bright lights, the anxiety, and, above all, the extreme loneliness she felt. I asked her to close her eyes and to remember what it had felt like to give birth as a teenage girl, still just a child herself. Quietly, as Bethany's head was bent in prayer, I began to describe how the doctor handed her newborn son into Jesus' hands, and how excited Jesus was to hold him! He lifted up her baby as if offering him to his Father. "You are fearfully and wonderfully made!" Jesus said (see Ps 139:14). I described Jesus' joy and excitement.

I asked Bethany to imagine Jesus holding her son close to his heart and walking around the bed toward her. I asked her imagine Jesus placing the boy in her arms. After a few moments, tears began to stream down Bethany's face as she saw herself holding her son for the very first time, looking at his face, hugging him to her heart. Very softly I said, "Jesus is now leaning over you. He has a message for you, a word that is only for you and no one else." Quietly I waited in prayer, trusting that Jesus would touch her heart. After a while, I told her that Jesus had blessed her boy that day in the hospital and was always walking with him, since she could not be by his side. I assured her that she could return to this moment at any time to be near Jesus and her oldest son.

After we finished our prayer time together, I asked Bethany if she wanted to share what Jesus had said to her. After a long pause, Bethany looked at me with a new peace in her eyes and said with tentative joy, "Jesus said to me, 'You are a good mother.'" I am always amazed at what Julian of Norwich would call the "courtesy" of God when he speaks to us in prayer. *Always* amazed. Never judgment, no threats, nothing to fear. Jesus knows the exact words a soul needs to hear in order to heal.

The following year, I was privileged to offer the same retreat and was happy to see Bethany again. I almost didn't recognize her. She had lost weight and her appearance was crisp and simple. The brightness in her eyes made her face glow. We caught up with each other before supper.

"I need to tell you what happened this year!" she said excitedly. Even though she looked joyful, I was not prepared for the abundance of God's graces flowing through her life.

"My three children got together and looked me up. I've seen them several times now! I still can't believe they would want to be with me," she said, her eyes gleaming with joy. Bethany told me all about her first visit with her children, what they were like and what they were doing with their lives. As I shared her happiness, God's power to heal and also to re-create, renew, and restore filled me with such gratitude.

Your Regrets Have Controlled Your Life for Too Long

Often unresolved regrets can express themselves in our lives through various unhealthy behaviors. Bethany had no idea how her addictions to alcohol and food were connected to the wrenching loss she had experienced in her teenage years. An avalanche of pain had buried her heart. Drinking and eating were simply ways to deaden the agony that was threatening to drown her in sorrow. But that escape route only led to a dead end.

Bethany's story is not unique. In some way, we all bury the memories that plague us. We hide in our work, perfectionism, surfing the internet, social media, sports, achievements, drink, drugs, food, etc. We often end up living on the surface, unsatisfied, empty, hiding our true reality from others, frustrated and afraid at what is happening to us. Over time, the passions of gluttony, pride, lust, greed, sloth, wrath, and envy can crowd our hearts until pieces of our lives begin to spin out of control.

Despite our best efforts to bury our regrets, they are always there, haunting us in some way. When Bethany asked me if God was angry at her for not having a job, she unconsciously expressed the deeper concern she couldn't face. Was God angry at her for doing all the things she regretted? She wondered if she was unforgivable. Her mind swirled with all manner of thoughts and memories: *I'm a failure. No one loves me. It was my fault. It is easier to numb the pain. No one can expect anything more of me. My life is over. I'll never see my children. It is okay to drink just a little more; after all, I have to have some happiness in life. I hate my family for what they did to me.* Sound familiar? As we've discovered, thoughts can keep us from finding peace and healing. We obsess over events that we regret. We go over our failures. We wonder what would have happened if we had made a different choice. We excuse, blame, label, judge, condemn ourselves or others. Thoughts, in the end, can hurt us.

Bethany's thoughts reminded her over and over again of her past failures. The woman who washed Jesus' feet also had thoughts of doubt, fear, and uncertainty, unsure of Jesus' continuing love for her: *I wonder if he will remember me? Will he know my face? Or was I just another person in his day, quickly forgotten?* You too may have negative thoughts around the regrets you have experienced. Like arrows piercing your heart, these thoughts can fill you with darkness and desolation, leading you to withdraw and to slink away from the light of Jesus' face. But when you access your story in the light of God's mercy, you can courageously look at the pieces of your life, accept them as your own, and let go of the darkness of regret in exchange for the light of Christ.

***

Let go of the darkness of regret in exchange for the *light* of Christ.

***

Jesus Remembers Only One Thing About You

Both Bethany and the woman who anointed Jesus experienced a personal, profound, and immediate encounter with Jesus that brought light into their lives. Many years ago, I also experienced a moment of grace that changed my life. I had struggled with dark memories that made me hate myself and wonder if God could love me. I even wondered if there would be a place for me in heaven (I was always a bit dramatic!). My struggles began when I was a child and had plagued my life until my early forties. I didn't think I would ever be free of them.

One Sunday afternoon I was sitting at the switchboard of our large convent answering the phone for our community. I was reading the sermons of Saint Augustine. No one else was around. Suddenly, I felt a strong sense that someone was looking at me. I looked around, but I was alone and so I went back to reading. However, the sensation persisted and grew stronger. As I tried to concentrate on my book, within me I heard unmistakable words that I will never forget: "What seems like an insurmountable obstacle to you is very simple for me to resolve. I need you to start looking at me."

In that moment, I had an inner experience of God's loving gaze upon me. My heart felt deeply moved, and an unexpected joy began to spill over into my senses. I heard God say within me, "As long as you look at me, and allow me to gaze upon you, it doesn't matter. Allow me to look at you and you will find peace and joy." A burning peace filled me for weeks after this experience.

I often walk by the room where this happened and, to this day, a sense of God's presence invades me when I remember that meeting initiated by God—a meeting that saved me. The moment I was healed. I continued with my struggle, but it gradually lessened until it disappeared. Instead of focusing on fixing the situation, I focused my attention on the face of Jesus.

Grace also changed the life of the woman who washed Jesus' feet. She received mercy from his hands, respect from his eyes, and hope for a new future from his words. Any attempts she had made to change her situation or improve her life before this encounter with Jesus had been only mildly effective. This meeting with her

Lord and Savior, however, made the difference between death and life. As she washed her Savior's feet, the woman's tears fell in loving devotion. With this simple but daring act, this woman's heart and life were changed forever.

Healing encounters with Jesus can produce memories of light that are strong enough to overpower the darkness of regret. Returning to these memories is like sitting on the floor of a sanctuary flooded with the light of divine glory. This sanctuary exists within each of us. Meeting Jesus flings open the doors of our hearts and floods our entire being with light. You, too, can have healing memories such as these. You may already have some. It is true that you cannot see and touch Jesus in his bodily form, but you can encounter him in your heart, and he is present in the Eucharist. You can detect a certain movement of grace within your spirit that signals the Lord's activity within you.

Experiences of God showing up unexpectedly in people's lives as told in this book are not extraordinary mystical visions. You have probably had such experiences in your own life. In these moments, time seems to stop. It's as if the heavens open and you can almost touch the power of God at work in your life.

God is pouring his mercy on us 24/7. We are the ones who often aren't awake, aware, and amazed at his gifts.

Exercise

How to Pray in Order to Meet Jesus

Just as one can't become an athlete or musician by practicing occasionally, we can't become athletes or musicians of the spirit if we pray haphazardly. Often what we desire so deeply in our life with God is perfectly within our reach if we simply persist in prayer.

This exercise is a gentle guide to prayer that, if followed consistently, will open your heart to encounter Jesus. To pray this way is to let the words and the way of the Lord be imprinted on your heart. It is to enjoy the Lord's love.

STEP ONE

To begin, withdraw from your sense-awareness of the world around you. Close your eyes. Leave behind your sight, hearing, feeling, and tasting—and go within. Become aware of your inner world.

STEP TWO

After you are settled, seek God in your heart. "The kingdom of God is within you" (see Lk 17:21), so seek your Lord there.

STEP THREE

Present yourself before God in your weakness, with your pain, your problems, your fears, and your secrets. Go to him as one who has no strength of one's own and needs to be carried on the way. Approach God with a deep sense of love. Try to draw near gently, without agitation, expectations, or demands upon yourself. Present yourself to God as a child. Say to him, "You are everything. It is only because of your love for me that I am here at all. Now I come before you in adoration."

STEP FOUR

Whether you feel the presence of the sacred or not, soak in the silence and feel yourself becoming more and more peaceful. Say the "Our Father" or a short spontaneous prayer. Say a few words of the prayer and allow the full meaning of the words to deeply touch your heart. Pause for a time of silence and then repeat the words again, each time allowing them to go deeper and deeper within you.

STEP FIVE

Patiently hold your heart in God's presence. Turn all your attention to him. As your outer senses become more and more quiet, you will receive a greater impression of his presence. Allow your mind to rest. If you start to notice what you are thinking, turn your mind gently back to look at the Lord.

The Light of Christ
Will Shine in You

Periodically, an encounter with Jesus breaks through our everyday, sleepy blindness and lights up our souls. The world becomes radiant and, like Bethany and the woman who washed Jesus' feet, we can't believe that we have been shown such mercy. We feel great joy in these moments because we know beyond a shadow of a doubt that Jesus remembers us only as he has made us.

But as the days go by, the radiance can begin to fade. We can't sustain the fullness of light from our experience of God's love. Our hearts begin to forget. We find ourselves once again experiencing fragmentation and forgetfulness. This is a normal part of being human. Even the saints experienced this fragmentation of the heart. Our senses, minds, hearts, and wills were given to us to know and to love God, and to make choices that would lead to us being united with him forever. Instead, we experience a scattering of our faculties, and it is sometimes difficult to even remember God at all. We wonder why life is once again so heavy and our memories so dark.

We can easily fall into the lie that we are supposed to progress, to get better, to one day be perfectly happy once we have healed and forgotten our past regrets. One straight line to eternal happiness. After all, God has forgiven our past and washed away our regrets, hasn't he? So why can't I? Why am I still ashamed? Why can't I look Jesus in the face with the courage of the woman who washed his feet with her tears? Why do I fear he hasn't forgiven and forgotten? Why am I scared that my regrets may one day be brought up before me? Is it that I haven't forgiven myself? Perhaps. That would be, after all, the classic answer.

With his divine power, Jesus can *transform* you in an instant.

One day, however, I was given a grace that I wish to share with you. This experience made clear to me in a new way that the Holy Spirit does everything that is good in me and in the world. He plants the seed for every virtuous act, no matter how small: a healing word, a kind thought, and a patient response. The Spirit guides the Church in issues of doctrine, and he inspires the smallest child to share a candy bar with a friend. As I sat before my spiritual director and explained this, I cupped my hands. "This," I said, "is all I have. A handful of ashes. This is all I have done, if the Spirit inspires everything that is good. The only thing I can do by myself is essentially broken." As I said these words I finally realized what had been my struggle for years. *I didn't want the ashes.* I wanted to know I was good and beautiful and important in God's Kingdom, that I had moved on, that I had been admitted into the elite group of "the good people." The more my spirit struggled to convince myself of this, the more I feared being found out, left out.

As I accepted the ashes I held in my cupped hands, I realized I am not supposed to move up the ladder and leave the past behind. My past is mine. *What I regret has actually made me who I am.* My struggles have become the sacred spaces of encounter with God. And to this day, forgiven though I am, all the regret I carry with me is a gift. It is a gift that pushes me to cast myself down before Jesus in adoration, reparation, and gratitude. For the redeemed, regrets are stepping stones to a deeper relationship with God. What I regret reminds me again and again of the face of Jesus at the moment he saved me. And his face—that blessed face—I wish to never, ever forget.

The Light of God Radiates from You

Both Bethany and the woman who anointed Jesus experienced deep personal shifts after their encounters with Jesus. The way Bethany carried herself at the second retreat, as well as her commitment to daily Mass, showed that something profound had taken place within her. She had been surprised by changes that seemed to come upon her without any effort. She felt as if she were living in another dimension. The words Jesus said to Bethany— "You are a good mother!"—were the words that raised her from the dead. An encounter with God can drastically change our lives in this way. When we allow God into our lives, he puts everything aright.

In his letter to the Romans, Saint Paul cries out in anguish about our shared human condition, "Who will rescue me from this body of death?" (Rom 7:24). His answer, and our answer, is a name, the name of a Person: "Jesus Christ." With his divine power, Jesus can transform us in an instant. This kind of encounter happens on God's initiative, not ours. We cannot make this encounter happen, but we can prepare the ground for it. Practicing awareness and watchfulness at the doors of our hearts will help us to respond to God's grace. In an encounter with God, we might experience repentance, a sense of urgency, a refocusing on God, a desire to do God's will, and a sense of joy that embraces the entire spirit. A grace-filled awakening can transform our spiritual horizons.

When we experience these awakenings, we often realize the ways in which we have turned away from God. But when we turn away from God, he doesn't pursue us with anger and vengeance. He follows us closely with truth and mercy. His mercy is truth, and his truth is mercy. In the face of this mercy, we realize that it was to our own detriment that we traded our relationship with God for things of lesser value. For long stretches of time, we ran along the path of life unaware of how much we were loved and how much we had betrayed that love. When this happens, we often feel repentance. Repentance is not a heavy guilt but a loving sorrow that makes the sacrament of Confession a need of the heart, a meeting with Jesus we cannot live without.

Many people also feel a perplexed uncertainty when our pursuing God catches up to them. If this happens to you, you may not know what to do next. You find yourself in the dark space between where you were and where you will soon be. In this moment you are invited to embrace a realignment of your inner self with God's dream for you. In some way you have chosen other things, other dreams, and other satisfactions in which to find pleasure. It takes a time of transition to relearn how to find pleasure in God's dream, in spiritual satisfaction, in the goods proclaimed in the Gospel that are often contrary to the logic of the world. This moment of uncertainty is a grace-filled time when you can make the decision to hear God's voice and to accept that he loves you. By placing yourself humbly in God's hands you allow him to recreate you.

When you allow an encounter with God to change your life, then all that you regret, all that has brought you pain becomes transparent. The light of God begins to shine forth through your pain, growing gradually stronger. You realize that everywhere and in everything you are in contact with a light that is stronger than this world. It is a life from another world. The gift of wisdom is actualized in you and you begin to see God through all things, with all things, and in all things. It helps you understand how God has been at work in your past and its purpose, even with all the meandering paths it has taken. You start to see the path that you should follow, learning from each event along the way, positive and negative. You begin to sense deep peace in the meaning of the events of your life and how God shows his power and mercy through all of them.

No path leads directly through darkness to dawn. But the dark sorrow of the past and the shame and remorse will slip away as you turn from them and look instead into the bright face of God. When you see God's face, you are taken up and out of yourself into what is utterly real. The world of regrets, as real as they are, is always less real than the saving mystery of God's plunge into human history, into every human being's personal history, including yours.

Exercise
The Seasons of Life

Take a few days to reflect on all of your past, the many seasons of your life. Like an artist who puts dabs of color on a canvas as she begins painting, the colors may not seem to match: light and dark, conflicting hues. Life is like that as we go through it. We can barely make sense of each dab of color individually, but seeing the picture as a whole takes time. It takes the work of a master artist who can blend all these colors together so that an image begins to emerge, the image the artist knew would come to be from the beginning.

STEP ONE

Make a "color list" of your life on paper. Identify the dabs of "color" that have filled your life. What are the bright hues? What are the events that are more in the shadow? Which ones are dark with sorrow and regret? Which ones are red with passionate intensity? Take time with this. Let your mind wander randomly over your life and take notes of your stray thoughts, images, people, and situations.

STEP TWO

When a painting is finished, the viewer can no longer distinguish the original dabs of color and where they were placed. All of them have been blended together in combinations and textures until all that remains is the whole. After you have created your "color list," spend some time reflecting on how the various events of your life are connected among themselves and in the larger context of the network of people in your life. Gently blend together the distinct colors of the seasons of your life.

STEP THREE

Finish the exercise by praying with Psalm 139.

Prayer Moment

God has only one painting he is trying to make out of your life. That painting is a beautiful image of Jesus, his dear Son. For some of us, the colors that become part of our lives are lighter, for others they are darker. But in the end the colors don't matter. What counts, what makes the difference, is the touch of the Master Artist who can blend any set of colors into a masterpiece of art.

STEP ONE

Take a moment to cherish the end of this part of your spiritual journey. Meditate on one or all of the following questions. Bring them to prayer and ask Jesus what he thinks:

What has been your most powerful experience so far? What in your life have you come to terms with? What regrets have you said goodbye to? In what way do you see Jesus differently? How have you changed? How has your future taken on more promise?

STEP TWO

Close your eyes and allow God, the Master Artist, to tend to the painting of your life, to blend the seasons: the living and dying, the gathering and scattering, the loving and the hating, tearing and mending.

STEP THREE

When an artist finishes a work of art, he or she rejoices in what has been created. But when parents rejoice in their newborn children, they rejoice in a different way. They don't say: "Look at what we have created!" They rejoice over the baby for him or herself. I think God rejoices in us in this way. Everything is completely due to God, everything is gift, but he admires us as though all the credit was ours. So let God admire you. Spend some time absorbing this amazing gift as if you were a child again. And when a surge of gratitude wells up in your heart, give voice to a heartfelt prayer of thanks.

BOOK TWO

Introduction

A tentative silence settled on the retreat house as the retreatants started their eight-day journey of silence. On the first morning, I woke up early. The sun was streaming through the curtains. Careful not to wake anyone else, I walked quietly down the long hallway to chapel. There I opened a Bible and began to pray.

As a religious sister, I make a yearly eight-day silent retreat, but this one was different. I was entering mid-life and the regrets in my life were becoming more and more burdensome. I was overwhelmed. Morning after morning, I brought my lifetime of regrets to Jesus and he invited me to turn my sad and frightened heart over to him. As memories surfaced, I prayed with the Gospels and encountered Jesus through different characters. Jesus spoke directly to me through Scripture and in my prayer meditations. His words, actions, and loving gaze brought healing to my deepest fears and regrets. As day followed day, the uncertainty I had felt in the first days of my retreat turned into peace. My heart began to heal.

I hope and pray that your journey with this book has helped you to slow down, uncover memories, and embrace the truth. Now you are ready to sit in front of the burning bush and, like Moses, to remove your shoes before God, soak in his love, and find the holy ground in the experiences of your life. You may feel like you don't need more prayer time. You may wish for more practical chapters with concrete how-tos. But this book is not the key to your healing. Jesus is. And you need to encounter Jesus in order for him to heal you and lead you back into life.

Allow *Jesus* to come into your heart.

I found healing through these meditations and, I know that you can too.

Allow Jesus to come into your heart as you pray with these meditations. Perhaps bring one with you to an Hour of Adoration or break each meditation up into different prayer times. The important thing is not *how* you pray with these meditations but *that* you pray with them. Feel free to skip steps or focus only on ones that are helpful. Take your time. In praying these meditations, Jesus will heal what is left of your sorrow. He will mend what is broken, and break open all the possibilities of your future. Jesus will show you his face, and under his loving gaze you will find peace.

Find Healing from Dark Feelings of Regret

"Do you love me?"
—JOHN 21:15

Peter played over and over in his mind those last moments with Jesus. He could not believe he had said with such emotion, "I do not know him!" Then Peter remembered the look. The look Jesus had given him as the cock crowed. Nothing in that look but intimacy, the compassionate gaze of one who knows and loves.

STEP ONE

Allow yourself to go within. Embrace the stillness inside yourself, the peace. Even if you don't feel it right away, it is there. Take a few moments for your whole being to settle down into that space in the center of your soul where God dwells. Even if you can't feel him or sense him, God is there, shining, giving, and loving. It might help to picture a bright light or a gentle candle in the center of your heart to represent God's radiant presence within you.

Step Two

When you are settled, read John 21:1–19. As you read, focus on Peter's experience. Imagine how Peter must have struggled with deep guilt and regret after he had betrayed Jesus. When you have finished, sit in silence for some time.

Step Three

Slowly read the passage again. When you finish, you may wish to use the following guide to enter into Peter's experience to find healing.

Praying with Peter

1. You are Peter in some way. You have experienced his dark feelings of regret at some point in your life, perhaps even now. Imagine you are Peter. Experience the dark mood and the regret he felt for betraying his Lord and Master. Sit with him in his deep remorse, in his hopelessness and regret. What is the heaviness like? Do you feel it in your very bones? Does the future look bleak and lifeless? When have you felt this way before?

2. Now imagine yourself in the boat with the Apostles. Watch the scene play out. You can be one of the Apostles or you can be yourself. You can watch what happens or participate.

Allow your imagination to take over as you make this Scripture story your own.

To put yourself in the story, it may help to read this imaginative account:

A voice called to them across the water, piercing the morning fog: "Friends, have you caught anything?"

"Caught anything? Does it look like we've caught anything?" Peter muttered to himself without looking up.

Again the sound of the booming voice sailed across the quiet waters: "Put your nets out on the right side of the boat and you'll find some fish."

"Come on, Peter. Let's give it a try," John said, as he pulled up the nets one more time and lowered them on the right side of the boat.

John and Thomas leaned over the edge of the boat as they gently pulled the net up. Nathanael, Peter, and the others held their breath; they felt almost too exhausted to even hope for a catch. The boat rocking was the only sound for several moments. Suddenly there was a tug on the net. A flash of silver . . . and within seconds the surface of the water was covered with fish dancing in the nets.

"Peter, get over here and help us!" John called, standing up and bracing himself. Nathanael and Peter helped him lift the nets over the edge of the boat, fish flapping everywhere.

"It is the Lord," whispered John so quietly only Peter would hear, but his words shot like an dart straight into Peter's heart. The man on the shore turned around and seemed to be walking away.

"No!" Peter called. This was his chance. An earlier catch of fish in the same place flashed across his memory (see Lk

5:1–11). A miraculous catch made at the bidding of the Master. He remembered the amazement and the profound sense that he was unworthy of being in the presence of this Rabbi.

Peter splashed into the sea, wading toward the shore. "No! Stop!" he called out.

As he stood on the shore he saw that the man had not left. He was bending over a charcoal fire, tending the food he was cooking . . . fish. Jesus looked up at him. The same look of mercy and love. "Come, Peter," Jesus said quietly.

And then the question he didn't expect, "Do you love me?"

3. After imagining yourself in the scene with the other Apostles, ask yourself some of these questions if they are helpful to your meditation:

What does Peter feel when he hears the voice of Jesus pierce his misery? How would you feel? When have you heard this voice? What is your response to this voice? Peter leapt into the water and splashed onto the shore in search of Jesus' voice. How do you chase the One who speaks a promise of forgiveness and new life?

4. Before ending your time of prayer, look for the face of Jesus in your heart. If you find imaginative prayer helpful, picture yourself sitting next to Jesus. Or you may simply ask Jesus for a sense of joy, God's nearness, or peace. Now hear the question Jesus asked Peter addressed to you: "Do you love me (*insert your name*)?" Listen to Jesus ask you the question directly, by name.

In the end, that is the only question you need to answer. Do you love him? If you do, then no matter what has transpired in your life, all will be well. If you love Jesus, then you will hear the words that were addressed to you at Baptism and Confirmation, at the beginning of your religious experience, your vocation, your ministry, or career choice: Follow me!

5. Conclude your time of prayer by speaking a prayer to Jesus in your own words. Or, if you need help finding the words, pray: *Yes, I love you. I want to love you more, but I see how small my heart is compared to yours, Jesus. Help me. Yes, I love you. I will follow you. I follow you because I need you. I trust you. I love you. I will follow you anew. Help me to be humble, wise, and completely dependent on you. Yes. Who else could I go to (see Jn 6:68)? Yes. I will follow.*

   Jesus has something particular he wants to say to you in response, just as he had something special to say to Peter. Lean forward and look into Jesus' eyes. What does he say to you? Write down whatever you hear or sense.

Journaling prompts:

○ Draw yourself with Jesus.

○ Write a poem or prayer to help you or someone else you know who has deep regrets for something they have done.

○ Finish this sentence: Jesus, I know now that you are

           .

○ Find photos online, in a magazine or newspaper, or draw something that represents first your experience of regret, then what your experience of Jesus in this prayer has been, and finally what Jesus is promising you as your future.

Find Healing from Suffering and Feelings of Powerlessness

"Behold, I am the handmaid of the Lord."
— LUKE 1:38, NABRE

The expectant and exultant chatter of the crowd had mercifully dropped to a whisper. The hammering had stopped. Now there was only silence. Mary felt as if her heart had stopped each time the heavy thud shook the ground. Her eyes closed as she felt a sword of agonizing sorrow rip through her body again and again. "I must stay here for my son," she kept telling herself. "Keep standing."

STEP ONE

Allow yourself to go within. Embrace the stillness inside yourself, the peace. Even if you don't feel it right away, it is there. Take a few moments for your whole being to settle down into that space in the center of your soul where God dwells. Even if you can't feel him or sense him, God is there, shining, giving, and loving. It might help to picture a bright light or a gentle candle in the center of your heart to represent God's radiant presence within you.

STEP TWO

When you are settled, read John 19:17–30. As you read, focus on Mary's experience. Imagine how Mary must have struggled with feelings of powerlessness and deep sorrow. When you have finished, sit in silence for some time.

STEP THREE

Slowly read the passage again. When you finish, you may wish to use the following guide to enter into Mary's experience to find healing.

Praying with Mary

1. Like Mary, you too have experienced feelings of powerlessness and deep suffering in your life. Imagine you are Mary beneath the cross. From within her look up at Jesus hanging on the cross. What does a mother feel when her child dies such a humiliating and tragic death? How do you feel about how life has turned out for you or a loved one? What do you most regret as you come to this prayer? Whom do you love that is now suffering? Do you feel responsible? Or powerless to help?

2. Now, imagine yourself next to Mary beneath the cross. Watch the scene play out. You can be Mary, or John, or one of the other characters, or you can be yourself. You can watch what happens or participate. Allow your imagination to take over as you make this Scripture story your own.

To put yourself in the story, it may help to read this imaginative account based on the accounts in the gospels of Luke and John:

The arms of the young disciple John were gently, almost reverently, wrapped around Mary's shoulders, giving her comfort and strength.

"Jesus is looking at you, Mary. He wants to see your face," John whispered in her ear.

"Yes," Mary whispered.

Mary remembered the words she had spoken to the angel Gabriel when he had announced the shocking news: Behold I am the handmaid of the Lord (Lk 1:38, NABRE). She raised her eyes slowly from his pierced feet to his crowned head. Mary took in the bruised and battered body of her Son; the One the angel Gabriel had told her would sit on the Throne of David (see Lk 1:31).

As Mary's eyes met Jesus' gaze, the words he had spoken to her as a child in the Temple came to her: "Did you not know that I must be in my Father's house?" (Lk 2:49). She had pondered those words her whole life since. She continued to think of those earlier, happier years. From his birth in Bethlehem to those first years in Egypt. In Nazareth, watching him grow, play, and learn to pray to his Father at her knee. She remembered Joseph, who was so kind and strong. The wedding feast at Cana when he had changed water into wine. Yes. Those had been days of miracles and laughter. Mary, like any parent, had great dreams for her Son. Now, standing at the foot of the cross, Mary reflected on how much had happened to her and to her Son in the thirty-three years of his life.

Mary recalled the words of Jesus to the crowds: "Whoever does the will of God is my brother and sister and mother" (Mk 3:35).

His words rang out in her heart.

"Yes," she said with more strength. The same "Yes" that ran like a golden thread through her entire life.

Suddenly she heard a noise. The clouds were threatening rain, and the chaos of the crowd was increasing. But Mary had heard her Son. Jesus struggled to call her from the cross, "Woman." It was so soft, in that gentle, respectful tone of voice he reserved for her alone. "Woman."

"Yes," Mary responded, her face straining up toward his.

"Here is your son," Jesus said as he turned his eyes to John. Looking at John, Jesus gasped, "Here is your mother."

Aware of the great goodbye now imminent, Mary looked slowly from Jesus to John and then to the crucified thieves beside Jesus. Then she turned to the jeering crowd for the first time.

"Yes," Mary whispered with tears in her eyes but a new strength in her heart. "Behold I am the handmaid of the Lord" (Lk 1:38, NABRE).

3. Stand in front of the cross and bring all the crosses in your life before Jesus. Take some time to consider your life's difficult situations, the heartbreak, and the tears. Now allow yourself to also cherish earlier, happier memories. Hold them gently as Mary did. Allow Mary to minister to you in your grief.

Despite the horrible reality that she saw as Jesus died on the cross, Mary perceived everything through the words of God's angel who had announced that her child would be the Messiah. She held fast to that promise. She held fast to her faith in God's power that she couldn't always understand. She held fast to her first response of yes to the angel: *Behold, I am the handmaid of the Lord.* When you are ready, make your own act of faith. Ask Mary to help you.

4. Picture Jesus looking down at you. He knows the pain you are experiencing. Tell Jesus everything that is in your heart. Speak to Jesus in your own words. Tell him how you feel about yourself, about the way life has turned out for you and your loved ones. Tell him about your anger, fear, or confusion. Jesus and Mary understand. Just like Mary, you have not had a clear road map through life. You depend on the mercy and providence of God. This leaves you open to receive a gift. Jesus has something particular he wants to say to you, just as he spoke to Mary, right in the midst of the cross of your life. What does he say? Write down whatever you hear or sense.

Journaling prompts:

○ Locate a picture of the crucified Jesus and paste it into your journal or on a piece of paper. Paste a picture of yourself and, on the same page, a picture as something that depicts the regret that you bring to this prayer.

○ Write a prayer entrusting your life to Jesus and place your loved ones in his loving, capable hands.

○ If you could have a conversation with Mary beneath the cross, what would you say? Write out what you would say and how you imagine she would respond.

Find Healing from Failures and Embarrassments

"Have mercy on me!"
— Mark 10:47

The Apostle James kicked a stone aside as he walked through the gates of Jericho. He was feeling pensive and barely registered the excitement of the crowd around him shouting, "Hosanna!" *Why had I asked for the highest place in Jesus' Kingdom?* James felt embarrassed, ashamed of himself. The sting of Jesus' words still cut into his spirit. James' thoughts were interrupted by the insistent calls from the beggars who sat along the road. He hurried to catch up with Jesus and the crowd around him as they rounded the bend of the road.

Step One

Allow yourself to go within. Embrace the stillness inside yourself, the peace. Even if you don't feel it right away, it is there. Take a few moments for your whole being to settle down into that space in the center of your soul where God dwells. Even if you can't feel him or sense him, God is there, shining, giving, and loving. It might help to picture a bright light or a gentle candle in the center of your heart to represent God's radiant presence within you.

Step Two

When you are settled, read Mark 10:32–52. The passage recounts both the story of the request of James and John and the blind man called Bartimaeus. The temptation would be to reflect directly on Bartimaeus, but as you read focus on what James' experience might have been like. Try to imagine how James felt when he was chastised by Jesus and when he saw the blind man healed. When you have finished reading, sit in silence for some time.

Step Three

Slowly read the passage again. When you finish, you may wish to use the following guide to enter into James' experience to find healing.

Praying with James

1. Remembering the times you have been filled with embarrassment in the face of failure, imagine you are James in the Scripture account. Imagine how ashamed he must have felt after asking Jesus for a high place in his Kingdom. Feel his confusion as Jesus reminds him and the other apostles that

greatness requires suffering and service. Have you felt embarrassed after doing something you regret? In what way have you experienced missing the mark in following Jesus? When have you felt as though you failed? When have you felt rejected by God?

2. Now imagine walking next to Jesus and the Apostles as they enter Jerusalem. Watch the scene play out. You can be James, or Bartimaeus, or you can be yourself. You can watch what happens or participate. Allow your imagination to take over as you make this Scripture story your own.

To put yourself in the story, it may help to read this imaginative account:

As James hurried to catch up with Jesus, he felt embarrassment overcome him as he thought again about what he had recently asked Jesus. James and his brother John had asked for top positions in the Kingdom when Jesus came into his glory. "And that went over really well," James grumbled. His request had led all the Apostles to fight with one other. Jesus had interrupted their bickering with words that James was still trying to understand: "Whoever wishes to be first among you must be a servant to everyone."

James finally caught up to Jesus just as he heard, "Son of David, have mercy on me!" The words rang out as clear as a bell even amidst the din and confusion.

"Jesus, have mercy on me now!"

"Quiet!" James called out to a beggar alongside the road. "Don't you see Jesus doesn't have time. He's on his way to—"

The beggar ignored James' words. "Jesus, son of David, have mercy on me! Please, Jesus, have pity."

Jesus stopped, and looked back to see who was calling out to him. Jesus looked at James, but James shrugged his shoulders as if to say, "I tried to stop him . . ."

"Call him here," Jesus said. James felt annoyed. So many people were calling out to Jesus, why was he responding to this one man? James walked back to the blind man, saying, "Well, get up. The Master is calling for you." For the first time he looked intently at the blind beggar whose voice had brought the crowd to a halt. He was dressed in dirty rags and a threadbare cloak covered his shoulders.

"Bartimaeus!" another beggar next to him said, "I think he wants you!" As James reached down, Bartimaeus jumped up and his cloak fell off and tangled around his feet. James knelt down and untangled the cloak and handed it to the beggar. Bartimaeus held it for a second and then tossed it aside. Haltingly, he started to half-run, half-stumble in the direction of Jesus. James observed where the cloak fell, knowing the blind man would need it when he took up his beggar's place again.

"What do you want me to do for you?" Jesus asked Bartimaeus. James saw a shadow of uncertainty cross Bartimaeus' face. The crowd waited to hear the usual beggar's request for a few coins or a bit of bread. Then a look of expectant joy flashed across the blind man's face as he proclaimed, "My teacher, let me see." A gasp rippled through the bystanders.

"Go," Jesus said, "your faith has made you well." Bartimaeus covered his eyes with his hands. Looking up, he slowly removed his hands and blinked. Then he blinked again. After a few moments he yelled, "I see! I see! I can see! He gave me back my sight!" The blind man leapt in the street, his joy overflowing.

3. Imaginatively stand before Jesus as you listen to Bartimaeus' request. Bartimaeus knew that the Kingdom of Jesus was about more than food and drink, power and glory. He asked for what he knew he really needed. Observe how you feel next to this person who knew that he needed God more than the air he breathed, the food he ate, and the water he drank. He could see with his inner eyes that Jesus had the power to heal his sight, so he asked with faith to be able to see. He expressed his deepest need. As you watch Bartimaeus ask for exactly what he knows he needs, you might realize you don't know what you really need. You might feel you still are seeking security, power, and comfort, even though these are temporary fixes that leave you unsatisfied. Let yourself cry out from the depths of your heart the one sentence: *"Jesus, I need YOU!"*

4. Imagine Jesus gently untangling your feet from the rags of your worries and regrets and the experiences of the past. Experience the firmness and the tenderness of Jesus' actions. When he is finished, observe carefully as he looks up at you and says your name. And then, "What is it that you want me to do for you?" Take as long as you need to respond to that question. What do you say to Jesus? Write down whatever you feel welling up in your heart.

Journaling prompts:

○ Draw a map of your spiritual life. Notice how you have gradually grown, how each step has led to the next, even steps that seemed to be taking you backward.

○ Find a picture of Jesus and paste it into your journal. Write a prayer of trust next to it or the words, *"Jesus, I need YOU!"*

○ Write an answer to this question from Jesus to you:
"What do you want me to do for you?"

Find Healing from Feelings of Unworthiness and Fear of Rejection

"I must stay at your house today."
— LUKE 19:5

The town's inhabitants poured out onto the streets as soon as the news began to spread that the miracle-working Rabbi from Nazareth was passing through. "I heard he restored the sight of a blind man in Jericho!" one woman said. All of the people chattered excitedly with one another as they hurried to the edge of town. Anticipation filled the air. Zacchaeus watched quietly from his tree-top perch.

STEP ONE

Allow yourself to go within. Embrace the stillness inside yourself, the peace. Even if you don't feel it right away, it is there. Take a few moments for your whole being to settle down into that space in the center of your soul where God dwells. Even if you can't feel him or sense him, God is there, shining, giving, and loving. It might help to picture a bright light or a gentle candle in the center of your heart to represent God's radiant presence within you.

STEP TWO

When you are settled, read the story of Zacchaeus in Luke 19:1–10. As you read, focus your attention on the experience of Zacchaeus. Imagine his nervousness and feelings of unworthiness when Jesus asked to go to his house. When you have finished reading, sit in silence for some time.

STEP THREE

Slowly read the passage again. When you finish, you may wish to use the following guide to enter into Zacchaeus' experience to find healing.

Praying with Zacchaeus

1. All of us have experienced times when we were on the fringes of activity. We feel left out, unnoticed, somehow unworthy. Imagine you are Zacchaeus and experience how he felt as Jesus approached him and looked up into the tree he had climbed. Was Zacchaeus worried, anxious? Did he expect rejection? Experience what he felt when Jesus told him he wanted to go to his house for dinner. Have you ever

experienced the acceptance and love of God even when you did not feel you deserved it? What was that like? Do you feel unworthy of God's love? Why or why not?

2. Imagine yourself in the tree waiting for Jesus. Watch the scene play out. You can imagine yourself as Zacchaeus or you can be yourself. You can watch what happens or participate. Allow your imagination to take over as you make this Scripture story your own.

To put yourself in the story, it may help to read this imaginative account:

"Ouch!" Zacchaeus slowly moved his leg, carefully avoiding the offending tree branch. He looked around, worried someone would notice him. But everyone was too busy waiting in anticipation to look up and notice him perched in the sycamore tree. Zacchaeus carefully repositioned himself to stand on a stronger branch. Squinting to see further down the road, Zacchaeus could tell that the mood of the crowd had changed. Jesus must have arrived, he thought. He felt left out. Not just left out of the parade of welcome for the traveling teacher. He had felt left out for a long time. Zacchaeus wasn't welcome among the people in the town because he was a tax collector. He had betrayed his people, his neighbors, the synagogue. Regret welled up in Zacchaeus.

I wish I could meet Jesus. I wish I could get to know him, but he won't accept me. And there's no way to change direction now, he thought sadly.

"Steady now," he said to himself as tears welled up in his eyes. He roughly brushed his tears away as the noisy crowd moved in his direction. Zacchaeus pulled himself more closely to the trunk of the tree. "I don't want them to know I'm here. I just want to see the Master who teaches great thing and has healed people. I just want a glimpse of his face. That's all. Just a quick look, then I'll go hide out at home. Wait . . . why is Jesus stopping right here?!"

Jesus had stopped right beneath the tree where Zacchaeus was hiding. He reached out his arms to the children who had gathered around him for a blessing. Then Jesus looked up into the branches of the tree. When his eyes met Zacchaeus', Jesus looked completely unsurprised, as if he knew exactly where Zacchaeus would be. With a voice full of compassion, Jesus said, "Zacchaeus, why are you in the tree up there? Come down. I want to stay at your home today."

Zacchaeus caught his breath. The crowd began to murmur. Zacchaeus wondered if he had heard correctly. No one came to his house—the house of a sinner. It would make them unclean. "Come on, Zacchaeus." Jesus' voice was caring but firm. Zacchaeus looked at Jesus' face; it was kind. But the faces of the crowd around Jesus were shocked, angry, and upset.

"What? You're going to eat with him?" someone called out.

"How can he pass over us for this no-good, tax-collecting sinner?" another grumbled loudly enough to be heard.

Zacchaeus jumped down from the tree and stood before Jesus, looking him over suspiciously. What was the catch? What was Jesus going to do? Surely he was not serious. Zacchaeus felt trapped. Jesus had said nothing about his tax-collecting, his cheating. Nothing about his past. He had only asked to stay at his house.

"Let's go, Zacchaeus," Jesus said. Zacchaeus pushed to the head of the crowd, leading the Master straight to his home. He could feel that something new was happening.

"Wait a minute," someone in the crowd called out. "You can't go in there. Do you know what he's done?"

Zacchaeus looked behind him. Jesus was not responding to the angry taunts of the crowd. *No one has ever cared this much for me before,* Zacchaeus thought. He stood a little taller.

Zacchaeus turned to Jesus and said with confidence, "I am delighted you are coming to my home today. In your honor, I will give half my property to the poor."

3. Picture yourself sitting in the tree waiting for Jesus. Bring to mind your own life. What is the "tree" you're hiding in? What things or people do you feel you've irretrievably lost because of choices you've made? Like Zacchaeus, do you bear other peoples' accusations and experience exclusion? What do you hope others don't find out about you? What are you pretending never happened? Write down your thoughts and feelings if you feel inspired.

4. Now, imagine Jesus stopping beneath the tree where you are sitting. See Jesus look straight into your eyes. "I want to stay in your heart today," he tells you. What do you feel when you hear those words? Excited? Ashamed? Afraid? Resentful? Whatever it is, don't be afraid. Jump down "out of your tree" and tell him how you feel. If you feel inspired, invite him into your heart just as it is. If voices within your own spirit or from others around you try to convince you that Jesus should not or would not want to come to abide with you, stand a little taller. Look right into his face. What

does Jesus' face look like? What do you want to tell him? Promise him?

5. Picture yourself in Zacchaeus' home that night at his dinner party with Jesus. Look around and see who else is there: tax collectors, friends of Zacchaeus. . . Observe how comfortable Jesus is as he dines with them. Tell Jesus how you feel sharing a meal with them and with him. What movements do you feel within your spirit? Talk to Jesus about the decisions you've made in your life that you regret. If you are comfortable, imagine yourself silently resting your head for a while on Jesus' heart as did the Apostle John at the Last Supper. Jesus has something he wishes to tell you. Close your eyes and listen there, next to his most gentle and holy heart. Write down whatever you hear or sense.

Journaling prompts:

○ Collect some beautiful pictures of trees. Write a poem or prose about how Jesus finds us in the trees in which we are hiding.

○ In your journal, creatively draw the final words of Jesus to Zacchaeus, words Jesus wants to say to you: "Today salvation has come to this house" (Lk 19:10).

○ Write a letter to someone who may have been hurt by a decision you made. You do not need to send it. Or write a letter to God about this person.

○ Finish this sentence: "I am honored, Lord, that you are coming into my heart today. Look, from this moment forward I will . . ."

Meditation Five

Find Healing from Self-Accusation and Guilt

"Neither do I condemn you."
—John 8:11

The woman was afraid to look behind her. She was caught in a trap. The men who had thrown her down before the Teacher surrounded her, each holding a stone. "She broke the Law," hissed one of the men, "and according to the Law she should be stoned."

Step One

Allow yourself to go within. Embrace the stillness inside yourself, the peace. Even if you don't feel it right away, it is there. Take a few moments for your whole being to settle down into that space in the center of your soul where God dwells. Even if you can't feel him or sense him, God is there, shining, giving, and loving. It might help to picture a bright light or a gentle candle in the center of your heart to represent God's radiant presence within you.

STEP TWO

When you are settled, read the story of the woman caught in adultery in John 8:1–11. As you read, focus on the experience of the woman caught in adultery. Imagine her fear, her self-accusation, and her shame. When you have finished reading, sit in silence for some time.

STEP THREE

Slowly read the passage again. When you finish, you may wish to use the following guide to enter into this woman's experience to find healing.

Praying with the Adulterous Woman

1. All of us have felt trapped by our mistakes. Imagine you are the woman caught in adultery. In some way, you can relate to this woman who wonders if her mistakes have cost her the future. Ask her to help you understand what she felt at that moment. Experience her fear, her shame, her uncertainty about her future. What does she think as her eyes follow Jesus—the only one standing between her and death? What is in her heart as the crowd tries to pick a fight with Jesus about the Law of Moses, seemingly having forgotten her altogether? What was it like for her to be a "case study," so to speak, and not a person whose life had

meaning far beyond their arguments or what she had done?

2. Picture yourself standing before Jesus, and behind him the crowd of people holding rocks. Watch the scene play out. You can imagine yourself as the adulterous woman or you can be yourself. You can watch what happens or participate. Allow your imagination to take over as you make this Scripture story your own.

To put yourself in the story, it may help to read this imaginative account:

"What do you have to say?" a man yelled out. The crowd was waiting for Jesus' response.

"Yes, Teacher, tell us what we should do."

The woman looked around her. It was clear that she was a mere pawn in a religious debate, they didn't care about her. The one they really wanted to punish was Jesus.

"So, come on. What do you say?" another taunted.

The woman turned her eyes to the quiet stranger who would decide her fate: life or death. She shuddered, perspiration running down her back; each passing second in the hot sun was agony. The Rabbi looked around at the growing crowd. The woman wondered if Jesus was looking for her lover since the Law of Moses decreed that in cases of adultery both the man and the woman should be stoned (see Lev 20:10).

At last, Jesus turned his eyes toward her. The woman was afraid to look up. Finally, she raised her eyes, and Jesus' gaze seemed to look straight into her soul. She felt warmed with a sense of safety, as if he began to carry her fear. No one had ever looked at her that way before. She felt as if the crowd had melted away and she and Jesus were there alone. She immediately trusted him.

Jesus glanced at the growing mob, then lifted his gaze, looking far off, remembering words from the beginning of his ministry: "Blessed are the poor in spirit. Blessed the meek, the single-hearted, the peacemakers . . ." (see Mt 5:3–11). If they truly heard them, those simple words tested a person's intentions and desires. Sighing, he bent over, picked up a stick, and began to draw lines in the dust. He was so intent on what he was doing it seemed he had forgotten the rock-wielding crowd altogether.

"So tell us, do you agree with the Law of Moses or not?" one of the younger men in the group asked, uncertainty tingeing his voice. They had clearly been expecting an argument.

Jesus straightened up. "Let anyone among you who is without sin be the first to throw a stone at her," (Jn 8:7).

After a few moments of silence, the men turned around and left. The stones fell from their hands as they walked away. As the crowd left, the woman stood alone before Jesus. She had been a pawn in their strategy to trap him. Now that the game was over, they didn't need her.

"Has no one condemned you?" Jesus asked the woman.

"No one, sir," she answered quietly.

"Then go. Neither do I condemn you. But do not sin again." It wasn't a threat. They were the words of the compassionate One who could help her find the meaning of her life. He had given her new life in more ways than one. With his final words, he ushered her from death into life. He held out to her a future now bright with hope.

3. Spend some time imagining that you are standing in front of a crowd of your accusers. Perhaps you are standing only before yourself. Or you may see friends, family, and co-workers amidst the crowd. Allow the accusers' voices, emotions, and thoughts to flood you. Recall your own experiences of things you've done and now regret, episodes of your life that are impossible to sweep under the carpet because they are already known by too many other people. Do you struggle with an ongoing weakness that is uncomfortably visible to others? Or maybe you've made a mistake, slipped, or were rushed into a choice you now bitterly regret. Have you sinned but can't seem to accept God's forgiveness? Take some time in silence to think about how you experience accusations and guilt in your life.

4. Now imagine Jesus standing next to you. Feel the same complete dependence and trust as experienced by the woman when she stood before the Lord. From this humble space, speak to Jesus with all the rich texture of your experience: thoughts, feelings, and desires. Picture Jesus looking straight into your eyes as you are surrounded by your own accusers. Jesus has something particular he wants to say to you, just as he said something to the woman in this story, just as he would have spoken to the accusers if they had approached him instead of leaving. What does he say? Write down whatever you hear or sense.

Journaling prompts:

○ Draw yourself surrounded by your own "accusers" or "accusations"—Perhaps you can't escape from your own self-accusation and guilt or are surrounded by

things you've done or people who know your story.
Draw Jesus there with you.

○ Sketch a straight horizontal line on a piece of paper.
Place a symbol of Christ in the center of the line. Next
to this symbol place a symbol of yourself. To the left
of the line write or draw some things you regret at this
point in your life. The more we remember and think
about them, the more they define who we are. Take a
pair of scissors and cut off everything written to the
left of the symbols of Christ and you. Now to the right
of the symbols write words of hope, dreams, plans for
conversion and growth. Try to use words that balance
mystery and concreteness, trust and planning. As you
finish this exercise, choose three things to incorporate
into your life as you move toward something new.

○ Write a letter to your "accusers" that requests their understanding, compassion, and trust. Include what Jesus
is doing for you. You can burn this letter when you are
finished, keep it, or send it to someone who you'd like
to read it.

Find Healing from Fear and Disappointments

"Were not our hearts burning within us?"
— Luke 24:32

The banging reverberated down the empty Jerusalem street cloaked in inky blackness.

"I know they are in here," Cleopas said under his breath to his companion. "Peter!" he called in a loud voice. "It's me! Cleopas! Open the door. We've come back from Emmaus! We've seen the Lord! Let us in!"

STEP ONE

Allow yourself to go within. Embrace the stillness inside yourself, the peace. Even if you don't feel it right away, it is there. Take a few moments for your whole being to settle down into that space in the center of your soul where God dwells. Even if you can't feel him or sense him, God is there, shining, giving, and loving. It might help to picture a bright light or a gentle candle in the center of your heart to represent God's radiant presence within you.

STEP TWO

When you are settled, read the accounts of some of the experiences of the disciples after Jesus' crucifixion in Luke 24:13–49. As you read, focus on the experience of Cleopas as he was walking on the road to Emmaus and later returned to Jerusalem to notify the other disciples. Imagine the fear and disappointment he must have been experiencing after the death of his beloved Lord. When you have finished reading, sit in silence for some time.

STEP THREE

Slowly read the passage again. When you finish, you may wish to use the following guide to enter into the Cleopas' experience to find healing.

Praying with Cleopas

1. Cleopas must have been frightened and confused as he walked to Emmaus! Have you ever felt like all is lost? Imagine you are Cleopas, walking down the road to Emmaus after the death of Jesus. What regrets are you running from as were Cleopas and the other disciple? Where are you try-

ing to control your life? To fix a problem your own way? To redirect your own life without the presence and power of Jesus? Experience Cleopas' joy when he realized that Jesus had appeared to him. When have you felt a change from dejection to joy in a few short hours? How do you identify with Cleopas' sadness or his joy?

2. Imagine yourself in the room when Cleopas and the other disciple returned to the disciples who were in hiding. Watch the scene play out as they tell the disciples what happened. You can imagine yourself as one of the people in the room or you can be yourself. You can watch what happens or participate. Allow your imagination to take over as you make this Scripture story your own.

To put yourself in the story, it may help to read this imaginative account:

A servant cautiously cracked the door open, raised a lamp, and peered out to see who was knocking so loudly. "It's them!" he called over his shoulder, then quickly pulled the two disciples into the house where the Apostles were hiding.

Everyone started speaking at once.

"We saw Jesus!" Cleopas said excitedly.

"You saw him? So has Peter!"

"Where did you see him? What did he look like?"

"Tell us, Cleopas. What was he like?"

"Quiet!" said Peter. "Give them something to drink. They've come from Emmaus, that's a long journey. Let them catch their breath."

Cleopas sat down, took a drink of water, and then began. "You all know we left Jerusalem yesterday morning. I saw no reason to stay. Jesus was dead. He had died like a criminal. I couldn't believe I had given up so much to follow him, and then he died like that. I wasn't going to hang around in hiding. On the way back to Emmaus we were talking about what had happened, what went wrong, what we could have done, should have done. It felt so lonely out there on the road, walking back to our old life. We were trying to figure it out, to make sense out of it. Attempting to comprehend what our own lives meant after this devastating loss of Jesus. We were getting nowhere."

Cleopas paused and reflected quietly, then said, "We were getting nowhere until this man joined us on the way. There was something different about him. He was so full of joy. Peace flowed from him."

"Was it Jesus?" James asked.

"We thought he was just a traveler," Cleopas continued. "When we told him about Jesus' death on Calvary, everything made sense to him. Where we saw roadblocks and problems, he explained to us the mysterious plan, the designs of God starting with Moses, David, and Isaiah— and fulfilled now in Jesus. It gave me such a feeling of hope to think that what seemed like the end might just be one dark moment in a journey that the Lord has blessed. . . ." Cleopas paused and the room was in complete silence for a moment.

"We don't really need to understand this on our own terms but on God's," Cleopas continued. "As the evening began to fall, we stopped and ate together. I realized how my heart was burning like . . . like . . ."

"Like the first time we met the Master," Peter quietly broke in.

"Yes," Cleopas agreed. "But the stranger gave himself away when he broke bread and gave it to us, just as Jesus had done on the night he was arrested."

Cleopas put his hand on Peter's shoulder. "Peter, I think everything is going to be fine. I think everything is just the way it is meant to be."

"Look!" James exclaimed.

The room was suddenly bursting with radiant light, and their hearts swelled with joy. A figure had appeared. He said, "Do not be afraid. Why do you doubt it is I?"

"Jesus!" Cleopas exclaimed.

"Look at my hands and my feet. It is me—risen—here—with you."

3. As Cleopas walked away from Jerusalem in confusion and regret, his shattered expectations had become a wall between him and reality. Recall times in your life when things didn't work out as you had planned. Someone got hurt. Plans fell apart. Dreams were shattered through others' mistakes or your own. A good question to ask yourself in these situations is, "Am I certain that this wall of fear and disappointment is the whole truth?"

   ○ Write down or recall a situation in your life that seemed bleak but that you were later able to see more clearly.

4. Quietly imagine yourself with the disciples and the stranger eating supper in Emmaus. Watch as Jesus quietly prays and then breaks the bread, handing it to you with the words, "This is my body. Take and eat." Let the radiance emanating from the face of Jesus pour over you. Freeze the moment and soak in the warmth and light from around that table.

5. The same thing that happens at Emmaus happens at Mass. In the readings and homily, we can hear Jesus helping us understand the large picture of salvation history. In the Eucharistic Prayer, the bread and wine become, as at the Last Supper and as at Emmaus, the Body and Blood of Jesus. Bringing this mystery to mind, sit for a moment in quiet peace. When you are ready, overlay the image of light and warmth in that Emmaus house where Cleopas and the disciple were at supper with Jesus onto your experience of the Mass. Let them merge together. Ask God to help you to see the mystery of the Mass—and the mystery of your life—as he sees them.

As you pray, experience the same amazement Cleopas had felt; your view of events is not how *God* sees them. Watch for the stirring of your spirit, the promise of a hope you could never have entertained without God's help. This hope draws you to Jesus in the Eucharist and is fueled by Jesus' real presence in the Eucharist. And this joy will propel you into the darkness to announce that "Jesus is alive!"

And you also have been risen from the dead!

Journaling prompts:

○ After participating in the Mass, call to mind someone in your life who is struggling to find hope and meaning. Reflect on the words you would use to tell them that Jesus is alive, and in him they can find new life and joy.

○ Write your own prayer of thanksgiving for the gift of the Eucharist. Try bringing it with you to Mass to pray after receiving Communion.

○ Make a list of your questions and regrets about life and bring one of these with you to Mass. Listen carefully during the Liturgy of the Word to see what wisdom you can receive to help you. Speak to Jesus about it after Communion.

Conclusion

Take a moment to honor the journey you have made with this book. It is not easy to open up your regrets, to pray with them, and to ask the Lord for healing. You have done something courageous.

You may feel like you have not worked hard enough. Or you don't feel enough healing has taken place. Perhaps you wonder why you still feel regret weighing you down. Don't worry. Your journey of healing has just begun and it will continue, opening you to wider and brighter horizons.

Jesus *will* heal you. Continue to wait for him.

Closing Prayer Meditation

One summer, as I entered into my annual retreat, a strong image came to me in prayer. When I shared the image with my spiritual director for those eight days I said, "I feel like I'm sitting on the edge of a reservoir. I'm beginning to realize that the reservoir of my life has been a closed place. It is constricted and small. And the water is starting to empty out! I'm feeling afraid."

During those days of quiet prayer I watched as my reservoir drained completely. At a certain point in my prayer, the Holy Spirit helped me to see that there was an ocean outside my reservoir. As I hung my feet over the side, my heart began to leap with joy at the possibility of sailing into the broad ocean where the sun scattered diamonds of light on the waves.

Your journey of *healing* has just begun.

This image and time of prayer marked a transition for me. As I looked forward at God's future for me, I saw no answers, no plans, and no dreams. But I was sure that God had a plan for me in his heart. And that was enough.

This closing prayer meditation will help you to embrace the incompleteness and the possibility that is the journey of healing.

STEP ONE

Find a quiet place to sit and pray. Take a few minutes to just sit in silence until your mind stops racing. Ask the Holy Spirit to inspire this time of prayer.

STEP TWO

Imagine you are in a boat on a man-made reservoir. Your boat glides across the surface of the water. You feel small, cramped, without horizons and possibilities. This reservoir represents your life up until this point. Your efforts, your accomplishments, your regrets, your mistakes, your hopes and dreams and plans. You have been sailing around this body of water all your life. It is yours.

STEP THREE

Now, imagine you notice something different today, an unusual movement on the water. As you carefully move to one of the edges of the reservoir, you realize that where the water used to end, a waterfall now appears. The water in the reservoir is spilling over the edge into a great ocean. The sunlight dances on the surface of the water, teeming with life and delight. Everything that you have built in your life is, like the water, spilling over the edge. The accumulation of a lifetime's experiences is now escaping and the water is draining from the reservoir. It seems dangerously low. How does this make you feel? Afraid? Hopeful? Excited? As you watch the water spilling out of the reservoir, allow yourself to explore your emotions.

STEP FOUR

And then your boat hits bottom. As the sun beats down on the empty reservoir, you see the mud hardening into dry, caked dirt. Looking around, you see other boats that have been yours: anchors, ropes, sails, and more, all strewn around, lying under the merciless sun on the bottom of the basin. What had been your wealth is now your loss. Take some time to be in this space.

STEP FIVE

When you are ready, walk to the edge of the reservoir. Sit down there, at the end of the world as you have known it, with your life as you have lived it. Look out over the ocean, an ocean you cannot reach on your own. As you sit in silence, allow yourself to be drawn by the ocean. Gradually allow yourself to feel a desire stirring within you to leave the reservoir and all that lies on the barren surface. The ocean before you is so overwhelming it paralyzes you, and yet at the same time it elicits from your heart a deep yearning to plunge into its waters. Feel the eagerness grow to launch out on the limitless seas. Cherish this tentative belief that your future will be different from your past. Let the yearning grow. Imagine that a rope is thrown to this yearning in your soul, a bridge built by the Holy Spirit in response to the earnestness of your desire. Return to this place until its beauty washes away the darkness of your regrets.

STEP SIX

Turn around and look once more at your "possessions" lying about you. Without water, they are useless to you. Look at all the experiences, accomplishments, belongings, relationships, and decisions, some of which you may now regret. They are all part of who you have been. They are woven into the fabric of your life and history. The way they have affected you and called out something greater from you has made you who you are. Spend some time remembering them, gently take them in, and let them be what they are.

Then turn and face the ocean once more with this prayer:

"I will stay here, Lord, waiting, ready for you to bring me to the ocean of your delight. When you come, I will be here, ready and waiting."

Dear Reader,

I hope that this journey we have shared has helped you to reclaim your regrets and to see your life, even the great disappointments and pain, in the light of God's great love for you.

As I grow older, I often think of my dear friend Sister Augusta. When she died at 102 years of age, she had been my sister in the convent for forty years. She was from Italy, and had come to the United States in the early 1960s. She had been an accomplished seamstress. She loved knitting socks, sweaters, and her famous hats. Sister Augusta had an old woolen slip. Every year she would take it apart, washing the wool thoroughly, and, after the wool had dried, needles in hand, she would knit the slip once more, creating it anew.

I love that image. When I finished my second year of walking through the deserts of my regrets—so many dark memories and sorrows—I felt that Jesus had "undone" me. I felt washed clean and remade anew. I sensed that as I moved forward he would help me pick up any lost stitches that remained, confident that he has my entire life safely in his hands.

My friend, I know that God will gather the stray threads of your life also and weave them into a beautiful tapestry. When you are able to see the mystery and wonder of God's work in your life precisely through what you most regret, you will know you have experienced healing. Moses lived in insignificance for years in the desert after fleeing Egypt because of his mistakes. But had Moses never left, he might have never been ready to lead his people out of Egypt when he was called upon by God. You, too, will see that your holy calling runs right through what you most regret and into the mission God now entrusts to you.

You will be in my prayers,

Sister Kathryn

Discussion Questions

Readers may choose to use these questions on their own or with a group. Three sets of discussion questions are provided for each of the four parts. Groups may choose one of the sets of questions to share on, or select a few questions from each set, or do all the sets in consecutive group meetings. Because the nature of this book touches on personal topics, your group may determine that some questions are better shared while others may be used for personal reflection.

The *Chapter Questions* are the least personal and can be used in groups as they revolve around the material presented. The *Meditation Questions* are also well-suited for group sharing as they open up a faith-sharing experience based on the Scripture. The *Sharing on the Exercises* and *Prayer Moments* questions require the most personal disclosure. However, these questions also could be appropriate for group sharing if your group has developed trust with one another.

Part One

God's First Promise to You:
I want to throw you a party

Chapter Questions

1. Do you have a sacred memory created by an experience similar to Jake's? How can you preserve that memory in your spiritual life?

2. Have you experienced "patterns beneath the regrets" in your life? How would you explain them in your own words?

Meditation on the Prodigal Son

1. What details about the parable were new to you? How did they affect your understanding of the parable's meaning?

2. With which character do you relate most in the parable?

3. Was there an aspect of the story to which you found yourself unexpectedly attracted?

4. Do you feel like a runaway in some aspect of your life?

5. When you look into the Father's eyes in this meditation, what do you see? If a party were thrown in heaven for you right now, what would it be like?

Sharing on Exercises and Prayer Experiences

1. What new images or experiences came to you when doing the exercises and prayer moments? Which exercise or prayer experience created the greatest shift?

2. Did you experience any resistance to the exercises or prayer experiences? If so, why?

3. What treasures from the exercises and prayer experiences will you carry with you as you move forward?

Part Two

God's Second Promise to You:
Look at me, and you will know who you are.

Chapter Questions

1. Did the story of Angie bring to mind an early memory that has had a lasting effect on your life? What have been the consequences of that experience?

2. Can you think of a time that you "told yourself a story" that was almost a reliving of the meaning of an experience you had as a young child?

3. If you tried any of the exercises that the author led Angie through (pp. 146–47), what did you discover about the nature of thoughts and the power of prayer? Did it have any effect on the practical experiences of your life?

Meditation on the Woman Bent Double

1. What details about the gospel story were new to you? How did they affect your understanding of the story's meaning?

2. Which character do you relate to most?

3. Was there an aspect of the story to which you found yourself unexpectedly attracted?

4. Do you feel like the woman bent double in some aspect of your life?

5. Have you ever experienced the healing touch of mercy and grace in your life in a particularly meaningful way?

Sharing on Exercises and Prayer Experiences

1. What new images or experiences came to you when doing the exercises and prayer moments? Which exercise or prayer experience created the greatest shift?

2. Did you experience any resistance to the exercises or prayer experiences? If so, why?

3. What treasures from the exercises and prayer experiences will you carry with you as you move forward?

Part Three

God's Third Promise to You:
You see your failure, I see your future.

Chapter Questions

1. Have you ever had an experience like Bill when God "spoke" to you in a way that was so different from your ordinary way of thinking that you knew it had to be him?

2. What do you think about the concept of "getting out of the way" instead of "figuring out the way"? Has this been true in your experience?

3. Why is it so hard to appreciate ourselves as we are, with all our vulnerabilities? What would help us to do so?

Meditation on the Samaritan Woman

1. What details about the gospel story were new to you? How did they affect your understanding of the story's meaning?

2. Which character do you relate to most?

3. Was there an aspect of the story to which you found yourself unexpectedly attracted?

4. When you look at the newspaper, what changes when you frame the events in this way: each of these people is, in some way, looking for love? Are there areas of your own life that you now see as a cry for love?

5. What most impressed you about the way Jesus interacted with the Samaritan woman?

Sharing on Exercises and Prayer Experiences

1. What new images or experiences came to you when doing the exercises and prayer moments? Which exercise or prayer experience created the greatest shift?

2. Did you experience any resistance to the exercises or prayer experiences? If so, why?

3. What treasures from the exercises and prayer experiences will you carry with you as you move forward?

Part Four

God's Fourth Promise to You:
My light will radiate from you for all the world to see.

Chapter Questions

1. How have you experienced Jesus saying something unexpected in prayer? How were his words surprising, as they were for Bethany when Jesus said to her, "You are a good mother"?

2. Have you found it to be true that the way we look at ourselves is often how we perceive God looking at us?

3. In this chapter, there are three accounts of people who experience a personal encounter with Jesus that changed their lives. Have you had an experience of God's healing love? Do you bring it to mind often? Do you give thanks to God for what happened?

Meditation on the Woman Who Washed Jesus' Feet

1. What details about the gospel story were new to you? How did they affect your understanding of the story's meaning?

2. Which character do you relate to most?

3. Was there an aspect of the story to which you found yourself unexpectedly attracted?

4. What struck you most about the people at the dinner party? Have you ever been like the woman, worried whether Jesus would accept you, surprised by Jesus' recognition and love? What was that like? Did you feel the same movement of gratitude that filled this woman's heart? How do you typically show your gratitude to God?

Sharing on Exercises and Prayer Experiences

1. What new images or experiences came to you when doing the exercises and prayer moments? Which exercise or prayer experience created the greatest shift?

2. Did you experience any resistance to the exercises or prayer experiences? If so, why?

3. What treasures from the exercises and prayer experiences will you carry with you as you move forward?

Book Two

Questions for Each of the Meditations

1. What details about the gospel story were new to you? How did they affect your understanding of the story's meaning?

2. Which character do you relate to most?

3. Was there an aspect of the story to which you found yourself unexpectedly attracted?

4. Where did you experience resistance and why do you think this happened? What didn't seem to resonate with you and why?

5. What treasures from the meditation will you carry with you as you move forward?

My Friend,

To you who share with me a hope in ever-renewed beginnings, I extend a warm invitation!

Would you join me at **TouchingTheSunrise.com**? As certain as the sun's rising melts away the shadows of night, the absolute faithfulness of the Master Artist's touch always creates something beautiful of our life's broken pieces. At **TouchingTheSunrise.com** you can bring your unique history to the one story of how God is transforming everything with his own beauty.

At **TouchingTheSunrise.com** you'll find support for your journey through life's wounding struggles: free resources and downloads, courses and retreats, meditations and reflections, a free Facebook group where I offer ongoing reflections and opportunities to touch the sunrise right where you are. Here you will discover a sacred space where you can meet the Lord and find others who are growing in holiness in all their wounded places.

Come and find the promise on the lips of Zechariah fulfilled for you:

> By the tender mercy of our God,
> the dawn from on high will break upon us,
> to give light to those who sit in darkness and in the shadow
> of death,
> to guide our feet into the way of peace.
>
> LUKE 1:78–79, NRSV

The Dawn from on High is breaking upon us, a daily miracle, an hourly grace.

I hope to see you at **TouchingTheSunrise.com**.

Sr. Kathryn Hermes, FSP

TouchingTheSunrise.com
SrKathrynHermes.com

Pauline
BOOKS & MEDIA

A mission of the Daughters of St. Paul

As apostles of Jesus Christ, evangelizing today's world:

We are CALLED to holiness
by God's living Word and Eucharist.

We COMMUNICATE the Gospel message
through our lives and through all
available forms of media.

We SERVE the Church
by responding to the hopes and needs
of all people with the Word of God,
in the spirit of St. Paul.

For more information visit us at www.pauline.org.

BOOKS & MEDIA

The Daughters of St. Paul operate book and media centers at the following addresses. Visit, call, or write the one nearest you today, or find us at www.paulinestore.org.

CALIFORNIA

3908 Sepulveda Blvd, Culver City, CA 90230	310-397-8676
3250 Middlefield Road, Menlo Park, CA 94025	650-369-4230

FLORIDA

145 S.W. 107th Avenue, Miami, FL 33174	305-559-6715

HAWAII

1143 Bishop Street, Honolulu, HI 96813	808-521-2731

ILLINOIS

172 North Michigan Avenue, Chicago, IL 60601	312-346-4228

LOUISIANA

4403 Veterans Memorial Blvd, Metairie, LA 70006	504-887-7631

MASSACHUSETTS

885 Providence Hwy, Dedham, MA 02026	781-326-5385

MISSOURI

9804 Watson Road, St. Louis, MO 63126	314-965-3512

NEW YORK

115 E. 29th Street, New York City, NY 10016	212-754-1110

SOUTH CAROLINA

243 King Street, Charleston, SC 29401	843-577-0175

TEXAS

No book center; for parish exhibits or outreach evangelization, contact: 210-569-0500, or SanAntonio@paulinemedia.com, or P.O. Box 761416, San Antonio, TX 78245

VIRGINIA

1025 King Street, Alexandria, VA 22314	703-549-3806

CANADA

3022 Dufferin Street, Toronto, ON M6B 3T5	416-781-9131

¡También somos su fuente para libros,
videos y música en español!